Young People's Science Encyclopedia

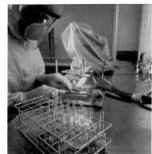

YOUNG PEOPLE'S
SCIENCE ENCYCLOPEDIA

Edited by the Staff of
NATIONAL COLLEGE OF EDUCATION, Evanston, Illinois

ASSOCIATE EDITORS

HELEN J. CHALLAND, B.E., M.A., Ph.D.
  Chairman, Division of Natural Sciences
  National College of Education,
  Evanston, Illinois

DONALD A. BOYER, B.S., M.S., Ph.D.
  Science Education Consultant, Winnetka
  Public Schools, Winnetka, Illinois
  Science, National College of Education

EDITORIAL CONSULTANTS
ON THE STAFF OF NATIONAL COLLEGE OF EDUCATION

Elizabeth R. Brandt, B.A., M.Ed.
Eugene B. Cantelupe, B.A., M.F.A., Ph.D.
John H. Daugherty, B.S., M.A.
Irwin K. Feinstein, B.S., M.A., Ph.D.
Mary Gallagher, A.B., M.A., Ph.D.
Beatrice S. Garber, A.B., M.S., Ph.D.
Hal S. Galbreath, B.S. Ed., M.S.
Arthur J. Hannah, B.S., M.Ed., Ed.D.

Robert R. Kidder, A.B., M.A., Ph.D.
Jean C. Kraft, B.S., M.A., Ph.D.
Elise P. Lerman, B.A., B.F.A., M.F.A.
Mary M. Lindquist, B.A., M.A., Ph.D.
Mary-Louise Neumann, A.B., B.S.L.S.
Lavon Rasco, B.A., M.A., Ph.D.
Bruce Allen Thale, B.S.Ed., M.S.Ed.
Fred R.Wilkins, Jr., B.A., M.Ed., Ph.D.

SPECIAL SUBJECT AREA CONSULTANTS

Krafft A. Ehricke, B.A.E., H.L.D.
Benjamin M. Hair, A.B., M.D.
Charles B. Johnson, B.S., M.A., M.S.
Raymond J. Johnson, B.B.A., M.Ed.

H. Kenneth Scatliff, M.D.
Eleanor S. Segal, M.D.
Paul P. Sipiera, B.A., M.S.
Ray C. Soliday, B.A., B.S., M.A. (Deceased)

Don Dwiggins, Aviation Editor

THE STAFF

Project Director   Rudolph A. Hastedt
Project Editor   M. Frances Dyra
Senior Editor   Jim Hargrove
Editorial Assistant   Janet Zelasko

Young People's
SCIENCE
Encyclopedia

Edited by the Staff of

NATIONAL COLLEGE OF EDUCATION

Evanston, Illinois

Volume 13/Oi-Pi

CHILDRENS PRESS ™

CHICAGO

Photographs

Page 2:   Skylab space station (NASA)

Page 3:   *Top to Bottom:*
Wheatfield (U.S.D.A. Photo)
Technician capping Abbokinase (Abbott Laboratories)
Spider (Macmillan Science Company)
View of Earth (NASA)
Space Shuttle (NASA)
Bahama coral reef (Macmillan Science Company)

Cover: Design by Sandra Gelak
Steel Workers (Inland Steel)
Indian Elephant (James P. Rowan)
Peacock (James P. Rowan)

Library of Congress Catalog Card Number: 67-17925

Oil deposits have been discovered on the continental shelves.   Gulf Oil

Oil well An oil well is a deep shaft that has been drilled down into the crust of the earth in search of oil. Oil wells are usually found in groups called *fields*. An oil well is normally made up of a shaft and casing, a derrick, and a pump.

Oil is one of the most important *fossil fuels*. It was first discovered in the United States when a well was sunk at Titusville, Pennsylvania, in 1859. This well was only 69 feet (21 meters) deep. Today oil wells go down to over 5 miles (8 kilometers).

Crude oil, as it is found in the earth's crust, is called PETROLEUM. It is classed as a HYDROCARBON fuel since its chemical composition includes compounds of hydrogen and carbon. While the main use of petroleum is fuel, many valuable by-products come from this compound.

Petroleum occurs almost entirely in *sedi-mentary* rock. It has, in rare cases, been discovered in other kinds of rock. Many theories have been developed to explain the origin of petroleum. Most agree that petroleum is derived from either oil-forming or oil-bearing plants and animals, or possibly from both. It appears more likely that most of the earth's petroleum was formed from animal sources. These organic remains are believed to have been deposited on the floor of warm, shallow, inland seas, and in shallow coastal waters around continents.

Oil tends to migrate from where it originates to a rock structure where it can accumulate. Often this accumulation takes place in the pores of sandstone or in the cracks and joints of limestone. Often, a layer of shale caps the deposit, trapping the oil and preventing its escape. The terms *oil pools* and *oil reserves* refer to these areas of saturated sandstone and limestone with an overlying cap of rock or shale.

NATURAL GAS is often found near petroleum deposits. When it is underneath the pool, it often exerts enough pressure to force petroleum up and through the casing of an oil well. In other situations, the oil must be pumped to the surface.

The search for new places to develop oil wells is one of the largest and most important tasks of the petroleum industry. In the U.S., exploration has concentrated around the continental shelf and the northern parts of Alaska. A huge oil pool was discovered in Alaska's Prudhoe Bay in 1968, the last discovery of such size to date. Over the years, oil companies spent about $50 billion to develop the Alaskan field. The discovery prompted construction of the 800-mile (nearly 1,300-km) Trans-Alaskan pipeline, which, in the early 1990s, carried about one-fourth of all the petroleum produced in the U.S.

H.S.G./J.H.

SEE ALSO: NATURAL RESOURCES, PETROLEUM

Ointment An ointment is a semisolid fatty or oily substance used simply for its protective effect or to hold medicine which must be administered locally.

SEE ALSO: DRUGS, SALVES

Okapi see Giraffe

Okra plant and cut fruit section

Okra (OH-kruh) Another name for this tall, stout herb is *gumbo*. It ranges in height from 2 to 8 feet (.6 to 2.4 meters). The FRUIT is a long capsule. When it is young, it is green and tender. Okra is used as a VEGETABLE.

Alternate simple LEAVES have palmate venation and may measure 1 foot (.3 meter) across. Yellow FLOWERS with red centers possess flower parts in fives. The compound pistil develops into a gelatinous fruit with many seeds. The capsule becomes woody upon maturity. Roasted seeds may be used as a coffee substitute. Stem fibers are processed into paper and textiles.

Okra is in the family Malvaceae. It is native to Africa and grown in the southern part of the United States. H.J.C.

Oleander see Wild flowers

Olfactory see Nose

Oligocene see Cenozoic Era, Geologic time table

Olive A shrub or tree that grows 25 to 40 feet (7.6 to 12.2 meters) tall, olive lives for several hundred years. It is gray-green in color with evergreen LEAVES. Green olives are the unripe FRUIT. When ripe, the fruit turns purplish-brown or black. Olives contain up to 30 percent oil.

Slender, leathery leaves are from 1 to 3 inches (2.5 to 7.6 centimeters) long. The leaves grow opposite each other on the branches, and their margins are smooth. White FLOWERS possess four petals, four sepals, one pistil, and two stamens. Sexes are separate. Following pollination, the ovary develops into a single-seed fruit that is classified as a *drupe*. Before the fruit can be eaten, it must be heated in lye and treated in a brine solution.

Olive is the name for the family Oleaceae. Propagation is done by stem cuttings or seeds. Italy and Spain lead in fruit production. Olives are also grown in the southern part of the United States. H. J. C.

Olive tree and branch

Olivine Olivine is an important rock-forming mineral. It is mainly found in BASALT. In GEM form it is called *chrysolite* or *peridot.* Its colors are various shades of green with rare brown tints. Olivine is a MAGNESIUM iron silicate.

SEE ALSO: MINERALS

Omnivore (OHM-nih-vohr) An omnivore is one of a group of animals that eats both animals and plants for its food.

SEE: BALANCE OF NATURE

Omnivorous see Animals, classification of; Balance of nature

Onion (UN-yuhn) An onion is a BIENNIAL herb related to the LILY. The bulbs are used as vegetables and for flavoring other foods. A chemical, *allyl sulfide,* escapes when the onion is cut and affects nerve endings in the nose. The nerve endings stimulate tears to flow from the eyes.

The onion grows to be 2 to 3 feet (.6 to .9 meter) tall. The stem is flat, disk-like and underground. The fleshy underground leaves surrounding the stem are white. As they grow and receive sunlight, chlorophyll is produced. In the second year of growth, a flower stalk produces a flower cluster.

Onions are propagated by *seed sets* (small bulbs) and by bulblets that grow at the top of the stem instead of flowers. H.J.C.

Onnes, Heike Kamerlingh (1853-1926) Kamerlingh Onnes was a Dutch physicist. He won the NOBEL PRIZE for physics in 1913. He was the first scientist to liquify HELIUM.

Onnes did very important work in CRYOGENICS. His liquefaction of helium led to the beginning of ultra low temperature studies. He discovered helium II. He found *transition temperatures* and *superconductivity* when he discovered that conductivity lessened at very low temperatures. A.J.H.

J. Daniel Willems
Black onyx

Onyx (AHN-icks) Onyx is a semiprecious stone. Greek myths spoke of onyx as the fingernails of a goddess which were turned into stone as they touched water. The name *onyx* comes from the Latin word, *oniscus,* which means "lined" or "partly transparent," as a fingernail. The lines in this stone are parallel. They are white with brown, red, or green variations.

True onyx is a variety of AGATE, which is a form of quartz. It is formed from the dissolved mineral *silica,* which has been deposited in areas of ancient lava beds or petrified wood. The colors are caused by the deposition of other minerals. Mexican onyx is actually miscalled because it is a limestone variety, frequently found as cave or hot springs deposits. This is sometimes called *onyx marble.* It is more translucent than the true onyx.

Onyx is easily carved and takes a high polish. It is used as jewelry, ornamental stonework, mantles, and pillars. J. A. D.

SEE ALSO: GEM, QUARTZ

Opal (OH-puhl) The opal is one of the main precious stones. It has been mined for thousands of years for use as a jewel. Long ago, people thought the opal had magic powers. Some thought it brought bad luck, but the Romans wore opals as good-luck charms. At the present time, Mexico and Australia produce the best opals, but the stone can also be found in many other parts of the world.

J. Daniel Willems
Black and white Australian opals

The common opal has a body color of milky white, pale yellow, or black. The better opals are iridescent, which means they show shifting lights of reds, yellows, blues, and greens. Opals are a variety of QUARTZ. Their origins date back to prehistoric times when water, seeping through volcanic ash, dissolved the mineral silica and was then deposited in petrifying wood or rock cavities. The "opalescence" or iridescence of this gem, which is its source of beauty, is also its weakness. The lines of varying colors are actually fractures or lines of strain formed in its development. While these lines reflect light, they can also cause breakage in the stone. An opal cannot be cut into facets but must be polished into a rounded surface and carefully mounted.
SEE ALSO: GEM   J. A. D.

Opaque (oh-PAYK) Opaque means not TRANSPARENT to human eyes; able to stop light rays and other forms of radiant energy such as infrared rays by absorption and reflection.
SEE: LIGHT, TRANSLUCENT

Window is translucent; wall is opaque

Open hearth process As the use of steel grew rapidly in Europe years ago, large quantities of rusty scrap iron were created. However, there was no readily available market for this type of metal. Sir William Siemens of England, therefore, felt compelled to invent a furnace which would re-melt the scrap and turn it into new steel. He accomplished this in 1856 with the discovery of the open hearth furnace. In 1864, Emile and Pierre Martin of France improved the process. Today it is alternately known as the *Siemens-Martin process.*

The open hearth process was the one generally used in the United States for making a good-quality steel. In 1942, over 90 per cent of the steel produced in this country was made by this method. The quality steel is used for the better class of rails; for structural steel such as girders for bridges, buildings, and tunnels; for shafts, armor-plate, and heavy guns; and wherever steel is to be subjected to much vibration. In addition to the very high-grade steel produced in this process, open hearth steel has three additional advantages. First, almost any kind of iron can be used as the charge. The *charge* consists of the impure materials which are refined in the process. Second, large quantities of steel can be made at one time. Third, the carbon content of the steel can be easily controlled.

In this process the open hearth furnace, or *converter,* consists of a shallow, wide, saucer-shaped hearth and a low roof. It may be as long as 50 feet (15 meters) and as wide as 20 feet (6 meters), with a basin about 2 feet (.6 meter) deep. It is lined with either silica brick in the acid process or with magnesia dolomite brick in the basic process (the process used in the U.S.). The hearth holds the charge of scrap iron, solid pig iron, and molten pig iron direct from the blast furnace. Limestone is added as a flux. A *flux* is a material purposely added to unite with the impurities. The waste product is called *slag.*

Natural gas or "producer" gas is burned to melt the charge. Pre-heated air and fuel

Diagram of a large open-hearth furnace.

gas (at temperatures of 2800° to 3100° F. or 1538° to 1704° C.) enter from one compartment and burn above the charge, which is heated by reflection from the roof of the furnace. The hot waste gases heat a similar compartment as they pass out above the hearth. The compartments form a system of fire brick checkerwork. After about 20 minutes, the compartments are interchanged so that the direction of the incoming gases is reversed, offering great economy of heating. This change is called the *Siemens regenerative process.*

While the charge is melting, some iron oxide is added as a flux—to oxidize the impurities to oxides of carbon, sulfur, phosphorous, silicon, and manganese. The oxygen of the iron oxide combines with the carbon to form carbon dioxide, which passes off with the flue gases. Other oxidized elements combine with the basic lining and form a slag which floats to the surface of the molten mass. This also prevents further oxidation of the iron. Since no air is blown through the molten mass, as in the Bessemer process, there is less iron oxide and dissolved gas in the finished product. By using as much as 50 per cent scrap iron or scrap steel, the oxidation of the impurities is speeded up considerably.

During the process, samples of molten steel are taken out at frequent intervals and allowed to cool and solidify. An analysis is made of the quality. Such treatment would be impossible in the Bessemer converter.

From the late 1800s until the 1950s, almost 90 per cent of the steel produced in the United States was from the basic open hearth process. In 1954 the basic oxygen process (BOP) was introduced in the U.S. By the 1970s, less than 30 per cent of steel produced in the U.S. was manufactured by the open hearth process.

The basic oxygen furnace (BOF) has many advantages over the basic open hearth process. It can produce larger quantities of high-quality steel much faster and more economically. The basic oxygen furnace takes about 45 minutes to produce a 330-ton (299-metric ton) batch of steel. It would take at least 5 hours to produce an equivalent amount of steel in a basic open hearth furnace.

The BOF is a tiltable, pear-shaped vessel. It is loaded with a charge of scrap and molten iron. Jets of pure oxygen are passed over the top of the charge through a water-cooled pipe called a *lance*. The pure oxygen raises the temperature of the charge rapidly and oxidizes contaminating minerals. Recent modifications, such as blowing oxygen into the bottom of the furnace, increase the efficiency of the basic oxygen process.   D.L.D./A.J.H.

SEE ALSO: BESSEMER PROCESS, STEEL

Iron ore open pit mine   **U.S. Steel**

Open pit mine Open pit mining is often the cheapest, easiest, and safest way to remove valuable materials from the earth. COPPER, IRON ore, and COAL are the chief earth materials mined by the open pit method. A QUARRY is a form of open pit mine where rock is mined for building purposes.

Open pit mining is generally used in areas that are relatively flat and where the valuable materials are close to the earth's surface. One form of open pit mining that has been highly successful for the extraction of coal is *strip mining*. Although its operation is very safe and economical, it has bad effects on the environment. In strip mining, as much as 131 feet (40 meters) of *overburden* are removed before the coal seam is reached. This material is then piled into large mounds. Once the coal seam has been removed, the coal company might move on and leave a moon-like, barren landscape behind. Fortunately, mining companies now restore the land to its original appearance once the mining is completed.

Coal is not the only material that is mined by the open pit method. Copper and iron ores have been mined by this method. The world's largest open pit mine is the Bingham Canyon, Utah, copper deposit. Open pit iron-ore mines are common to the Mesabi Range of upper Michigan and Minnesota. Quarries, another form of open pit mine, are employed for the removal of such building materials as granite, marble, and limestone.   P.P.S.

SEE ALSO: MINERAL, ORE, ROCK

Operation see Surgery

Ophthalmoscope (op-THAL-muh-scope) An ophthalmoscope is an instrument used to look into the eye to find damage or disease. The back of the eyeball (retina), with its arteries and veins, and the optic nerve can be clearly seen.

The lens of the eye can be checked for clouding (cataracts), or the retina can be checked for damage to the blood vessels caused by DIABETES (diabetic retinopathy) or *hypertension* (hypertensive retinopathy). By using the ophthalmoscope, the condition of other arteries and veins not easily seen can be determined. In addition, the relationship of the optic nerve to the rest of the retina tells if there is increased pressure behind the eyeball from the brain (papilledema), sometimes the first indication of a brain tumor.   E.S.S.

Opiate see Narcotics, Opium

Opium (OH-pee-um) Opium has been used since ancient times. It is a narcotic drug made from the dried milk or juice from the pod of the unripe poppy *(Papaver somniferum)*. However, various useful drugs, such as codeine, morphine, laudanum, and

Opium is obtained from the pod of an opium poppy

After the baby opossums are old enough to come out of the marsupial pouch, they ride on the mother's back

paregoric, are obtained from opium. It has been said that opium has brought more relief to the world through its legal uses and more unhappiness through its illegal uses than anything else known to man.

Doctors use opium drugs mainly for the relief of pain. Every American soldier in World War II carried morphine (from opium) in case he was wounded.

Improper use of opium derivatives *(opiates)* can lead to drug addiction—physical dependence on the drugs. Heroin, obtained from morphine, is the most widely used drug in illegal trade. Continued use of these drugs may lead to inability to follow a normal useful life and eventually to complete physical ruin and death. *Methadone,* a non-narcotic substance, has helped some addicts to give up heroin.   H.J.C.

Opossum (oh-PAHS-um) The opossum is a *marsupial,* an animal with a pouch. Opossums are the only pouched animals in North America. This *common* or *Virginia opossum* is about the size of a cat and has grayish fur. It has a long, light-gray snout. With its long, hairless tail, the opossum can carry things or even hang upside down from a tree branch.

The opossum does not seem to be a very intelligent animal. Its only interests seem to be in keeping safe, comfortable, and free from hunger. It will eat anything—insects, fruits, other animals, eggs, or roots. The meat of the opossum is edible. When surprised by a hunter, an opossum falls into a state of shock

and paralysis and appears to be dead. It is fear, not intelligence, that gives it this trick of "playing 'possum."

Opossums belong to a group of marsupials called *didelphids,* meaning that the female has two wombs. There is no placenta, however, which would be the source of food for the unborn offspring. As a result, newborn opossums are very small, undeveloped creatures. A litter often contains more infants than the mother can feed. First arrivals attach themselves to a nipple and the late ones starve. The survivors grow rapidly and crawl out of the pouch and attach themselves to the mother's back, where they ride until they can take care of themselves.

There are numerous other varieties of opossum in South and Central America. Like the North American opossum, they are generally neither friendly, beautiful, nor intelligent. The opossum has survived unchanged and untamed for thousands of years.   C. L. K.

SEE ALSO: MAMMALIA, MARSUPIAL

Oppenheimer, J. Robert (1904-1967)

J. Robert Oppenheimer, an American physicist, was director of the research project at Los Alamos, New Mexico, from 1943 to 1945. His genius, inspiration, and leadership guided many scientists in the development and testing of the first atomic bomb.

In 1943 Oppenheimer was assigned to the special laboratory at Los Alamos, New Mexico, near Santa Fe. With the assistance of several thousand others, the first atom bomb was designed and constructed. It was successfully exploded in July, 1945. Two years later, Oppenheimer was appointed director of the Institute of Advanced Study at Princeton and continued to serve on the Atomic Energy Commission.

Oppenheimer was summoned to Washington, D.C., in 1953 to face charges that he had been associated with Communists and had strongly opposed the hydrogen bomb project in 1949. He was "tried" by the personnel committee of the Atomic Energy Commission (AEC). However, over the years his prestige increased, and he became a symbol of the scientist who strives to understand and accept the fullness of his responsibilities in the modern world. President Lyndon B. Johnson honored Oppenheimer with the Enrico Fermi Award

Optic nerve

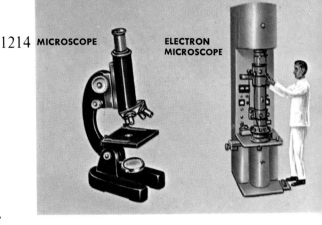

in 1963 for his contributions to theoretical physics as a teacher, an originator of ideas, and a leader in the AEC program.

Oppenheimer was interested in the problems of the day and discussed current issues with his students and colleagues. In his articles and lectures, he considered the relationship between science and society. He had purpose and conviction which were reflected in everything he did or said, particularly in his third book (1960), *Some Reflections on Science and Culture.* M.W.C.

Optic nerve see Eye, Nervous system

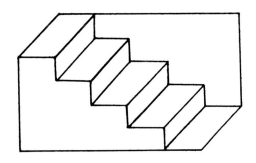

Are the stairs right side up or upside down?

Optical illusion The eye is a marvelous optical instrument, but sometimes the images formed by both eye and brain lead a person to a wrong idea about what the eye is viewing. An optical illusion is such an error in sense as well as understanding.

Some objects are mistakenly seen as changed. These errors may be in perception of shape, size, color, or motion. Besides illusions due simply to how objects are arranged, physical illusions can be caused by prisms, lenses, mirrors, and photography. Geometrical illusions are frequent. They are caused by the position of objects in the visual field. The symbols 333 SSS 888 when viewed upside down (888 SSS ƐƐƐ) seem to change. Observe the apparent size of the upper and lower portion of these symbols. Contour and shading give the illusion of depth. Contrast, perspective, and angles can also produce optical illusions. By using various combinations of illusions, animals through evolution and man through his art have developed the details of camouflage. M. B. C.

Optical instruments Optical instruments are devices which direct or control the passage of light. Other than the eye, a few of the common optical instruments are: eyeglasses, binoculars, mirrors, magnifying lenses, microscopes, telescopes, searchlights, periscopes, photoelectric devices, spectrometers, spectroscopes, photometers, polarizers, interferometers, and lasers.

In the 1500's and 1600's, the first optical instruments were developed, following the discovery of the glass lens. The earliest telescopes and microscopes evolved because of the lens.

Eyeglasses are used to correct astigmatism, nearsightedness, farsightedness, image size, and the amount and color of the light entering the eye. Important uses of the spectrometer are in measuring wavelengths of colors and their angle of spread when passed through its prism and in identifying the chemical element emitting light. Interferometers measure wavelength, index of refraction, and astronomical velocities and distances. This is done by splitting two beams of light and comparing the optical paths.

Intensity of light is measured by one or another type of light meter. Photoelectric-cell meters convert light to electricity, and then the light strength is read on a dial. A laboratory PHOTOMETER compares a standard light source at a given distance with an unknown light at a measured distance; then by use of the *inverse square law,* the strength of the unknown light can be figured. Measurement units of intensity for light instruments are either in FOOT CANDLES or in the new units, *candelas.*

The speed of light can be measured by an optical instrument developed by Albert A.

TELESCOPE

BINOCULARS

CAMERA LENS

POLARIZED LENS,

WHEN CROSSED
WILL STOP THE
LIGHT

Michelson of the University of Chicago. He determined that light in a vacuum travels at the speed of 186,284 miles (299,795 kilometers) per second.

Some instruments use *polarized light.* This is ordinary light that has been passed through a device that makes all its waves vibrate in one direction only instead of moving in several planes. This is done by directing the light through crystals that have a slit-like molecular arrangement or else through plastic sheets coated with certain chemicals. Polarized light devices include camera filters, glare-reducing sunglasses, and car headlights. Biochemists use it in an instrument that measures strength of sugar solutions. Engineers who work with construction and manufacturing materials use polarized beams to reveal strains in glass and plastics.

SEE ALSO: BINOCULAR; CAMERA; GLASS; LENS, MAN-MADE; LIGHT; MICROSCOPE; MICROSCOPE, ELECTRON; MIRROR; PERISCOPE; PRISM; TELESCOPE

Optical masers see Lasers

Optics Optics is the branch of physics that deals with the laws of light in relation to vision. It covers the production, transmission, and detection of electromagnetic radiation of wavelengths longer than X rays and shorter than microwaves.

Geometrical optics is the study of the reflection of light, refraction of light, velocity of light, and lenses. It also deals with the theory and design of optical instruments. Physical optics is the study of polarization of light, interference, and diffraction. Wave mechanics and quantum optics include the study of line spectra, color, thermal radiation, intensity, photometry, and wave equations.   M. B. C.
SEE ALSO: ELECTROMAGNETIC SPECTRUM; LENS, MAN-MADE

Optometry (ahp-TAHM-uh-tree) Optometry is a profession specializing in the protection and improvement of vision. The optometrist is one who practices the art and science of vision care. He is trained and licensed to make tests to determine the person's visual skills, especially in relation to his specific needs. When visual errors are found, he prescribes and provides any corrective lenses or visual training needed for adequate and comfortable sight.

The roots of the profession of optometry lie in the development of research in physics, mathematics, and optics, as well as in physiology and psychology. Modern optometry, however, really dates from the 19th century, when such men as Thomas Young, Herman von Helmholtz, Eduard Jaeger, and others, were busily engaged in Europe in measuring the eye and inventing instruments for testing sight. The results of their research are found in the applications used today. Development in the field of refraction led to the refractive testing of the eye, or optometry, as it is now known.

The word "optometry," in the sense of "diagnosis of refractive error" first appeared in 1870, and in the next thirty years optometry slowly evolved as a specialized vocation. Two outstanding leaders in the United States responsible for developing the profession were Charles F. Prentiss, who campaigned for legal recognition of the group, and Andrew J. Cross, who devoted himself to the establishment and improvement of the optometric educational facilities. By 1901, the first state law regulating the practice of optometry was passed in Minnesota. At the present time, the practice of optometry is recognized and regulated by state

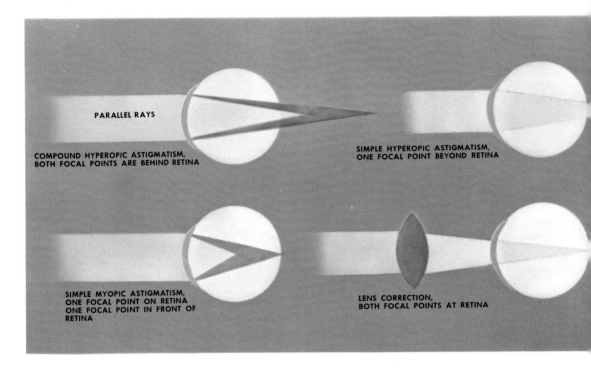

PARALLEL RAYS

COMPOUND HYPEROPIC ASTIGMATISM,
BOTH FOCAL POINTS ARE BEHIND RETINA

SIMPLE HYPEROPIC ASTIGMATISM,
ONE FOCAL POINT BEYOND RETINA

SIMPLE MYOPIC ASTIGMATISM,
ONE FOCAL POINT ON RETINA
ONE FOCAL POINT IN FRONT OF
RETINA

LENS CORRECTION,
BOTH FOCAL POINTS AT RETINA

laws in every state in the Union and by federal law in the District of Columbia.

Optometry has encompassed new responsibilities in helping people's eyes to function properly under the increasing strain of modern living. The optometrist also provides an extremely important service by recognizing all abnormal eye pathology and referring the person to an *ophthalmologist* (a medical doctor who can do eye surgery).

Contact lenses are optometry's contribution to many whose careers in athletics, aviation, on the stage, screen and television, depend on being able to see safely or to present the most aesthetic appearance.

Telescopic spectacles have been instrumental in returning the near blind to usefulness by helping them to see more than was previously thought possible.

The use of visual training and orthoptics (eye exercise) in the correction of squint (crossed eyes) and in the development or re-education of the visual skills for the improvement of visual performances was also due to the influence of optometry.

Vision is only one of the senses, but people rely on it more than on all the others put together. Most vision problems are due to *refractive errors* or inability of the eyes to focus light rays in the proper way. Glasses are the most common remedy for these errors. By relieving strain and permitting the eyes to function normally, glasses enable the individual not only to see clearly, but also to see efficiently and comfortably. The optometrist normally gives his prescription for the type of glasses needed to an *optician,* the technician who grinds glasses to specification.

Faults of vision may be grouped into five classes: hyperopia (farsightedness), myopia (nearsightedness), astigmatism, presbyopia (aging eyes), and strabismus (cross-eye).

The condition describing a normal eye is known as *emmetropia.* A properly functioning eye refracts rays of light from a distant object (more than 20 feet or 6 meters away) so that the image is brought to a focus at the retina when that eye is at rest.

Hyperopia is a state or condition of an eye which refracts parallel rays of light to a focus at a point behind the retina when the eye is at rest. In this case, the retina intercepts the converging rays of light before they reach their focal point. Farsightedness is corrected by placing a convex, or plus, lens before the eye. The power of the lens is such that it will converge the rays before they reach the eye, enabling them to focus on the retina.

Myopia is a state or condition of an eye which refracts parallel rays of light to a focus at a point in front of the retina when the eye is at rest. In such a case, the retina

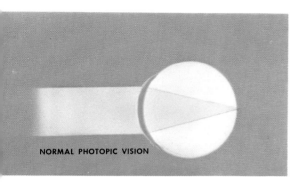

NORMAL PHOTOPIC VISION

Courtesy Society For Visual Education, Inc.

intercepts the rays of light after they have converged to a focal point. Nearsightedness is corrected by placing a concave, or minus, lens before the eye. The power of the lens is such that it will diverge the rays before they reach the eye, enabling them to focus on the retina.

Astigmatism is the most common refractive error. It is a condition of an eye which refracts parallel rays of light so that they do not focus at one point. In most cases, astigmatism is the result of the cornea not being truly spherical. There are many forms of astigmatism. The correction of an astigmatic eye is obtained by placing a cylindrical or sphero-cylindrical lens before the eye.

Presbyopia means literally "old sight." It is a state or condition in which the near point of any eye gradually recedes. Presbyopia is the result of a gradual hardening of the lens in the eye, and is universally present in persons 40 years or older. The addition of a convex or plus lens makes up for the loss in power and thus allows clear vision at near distances.

Strabismus is a Greek word meaning "squint" and describes what is commonly recognized as cross-eyes (internal strabismus) or wall-eyes (external strabismus). This is usually caused by eye muscle imbalance, and if not caught early enough in life and corrected (by lenses, visual training, and/or surgery), the person stops using one eye and becomes functionally blind in it *(amblyopia ex anopsia)*.

J.H.D./E.S.S.

Oral Oral means spoken and pertains to the mouth. In ZOOLOGY it refers to the same side of the animal as the mouth or mouth region.

SEE: ANIMAL

Orange see Citrus fruits

Orangutan (oh-RANG-oo-tann) *Orang* means "man" and *utan* means "jungle." Thus the orangutan is called "man-of-the-woods." It belongs to the APE family, and spends most of its life in tree tops, coming down to the ground only for water. An orangutan, if captured young, can be easily trained. Within weeks, it can be taught to eat, dress, and act well-behaved.

Some orangutans have reached the height of 4½ feet (1.4 meters). The males may weigh 100 pounds (90.7 kilograms); the females are usually smaller. In spite of their great weight, they travel very rapidly; for though their legs are little and weak, their arms are strong and muscular, enabling them to swing rapidly from tree to tree rather than leap as many other PRIMATES do. Their long, loose hair ranges from brick-red to brownish-orange, and their cheeks are wide and flat.

Orangutans are chiefly vegetarians, feasting on wild fruit, especially on the fruit of durain, shoots of screw pine, and fleshy leaves of various kinds. H.J.C.

Orbit The word orbit describes the path of any body that revolves around another body. The path is an ellipse. Some orbits are nearly circles; others are very elongated.

Probably one of the oldest significant uses of the word orbit refers to the paths of celestial bodies as they revolve around the sun. Earth and other planets move in specific orbits as they travel through the sun's gravitational pull. Planets with natural satellites are the centers of the satellites' orbits.

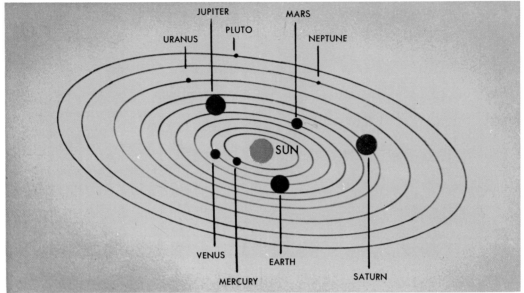

Figure 1—The nine planets of our solar system are natural satellites of the sun. All of these planets are many times smaller than the sun

An orbiting body may be a small body that revolves around a larger body. These two bodies have a common center of gravity, always located between them but nearer to the center of the system. In the earth-moon system, the center of gravity of the system lies under the crust of the earth. Orbiting bodies are referred to as satellites. There are two types—natural and man-made. Both the moon and the earth are examples of natural satellites. The Space Age has brought about the development of dozens of man-made satellites which not only revolve about the earth but other heavenly bodies as well.

Atoms also have particles which can be thought of as traveling in an orbit. These particles are the electrons which revolve about a nucleus composed of protons, neutrons, and other subatomic particles. At one time it was thought that these orbits were as simple as a circle. Now the paths of the electrons are recognized as three-dimensional orbits. If the path of the electron were traced, in time it would form a sort of "shell" around the nucleus. These paths are called *orbitals.*

The general laws of orbital motion were worked out by JOHANNES KEPLER. The "first law" states that the shape of the orbit of one body about another is an ellipse. The primary body is at one focus of the ellipse. The "second law" states that the line from the larger body to the smaller, orbiting body

sweeps over equal areas in equal times. The "third law" states that the space between the objects is proportional to the period of time for one revolution. H.S.G./A.J.H.

SEE ALSO: APOGEE, ORBITAL SYSTEMS, PERIGEE, SPACE TRAVEL

Orbital systems This is an astronautical term used to describe a series of satellites which have been placed in orbit around the earth to form a coordinated network. These satellites may have the same or different orbits. The satellites are usually linked to ground-control stations and auxiliary *readout* stations by computerized radio communications.

Orbital systems have several uses including relaying radio, television, and telephone signals from one part of the earth to another. Another system furnishes photographs of the earth from space to assist in weather forecasting. The military has several satellite networks to improve sea and air navigation and to provide military reconnaissance information.

SATELLITE ORBITS

A satellite must be launched into space and accelerated to a velocity at which the centrifugal force created is offset by the gravitational pull of the earth. The satellite will then go into orbit around the earth. As the altitude of the satellite increases, its velocity decreases, and its period—the time the satellite takes to circle the Earth—increases. A satellite remains in orbit until its velocity decreases and the gravitational force of the earth pulls it down into the earth's atmosphere.

The velocity required to put a satellite into orbit varies with the altitude at which the satellite will orbit. Satellites that orbit at low altitudes—between 300-500 miles (480-805 kilometers) above the earth—require greater velocities than those with orbits at high altitudes For example, a satellite in orbit 175 miles (282 kilometers) above the earth requires a velocity of 17,500 miles (28,163 kilometers) per hour to maintain the orbit. But a satellite in orbit 240,000 miles (386,240 kilometers) requires a velocity of only 2,000 miles (3,219 kilometers) per hour.

Several types of orbits can be achieved, depending upon the altitude, velocity and direction of the vehicle. Some orbits are classified by shape, others are classified by placement and altitude.

Circular and *elliptical* orbits are classified by their shape. A circular orbit results when the satellite is launched in a straight horizontal path in space. Any tilt to the launching path or incorrect velocities will result in an elliptical orbit. In an elliptical orbit, the satellite is closer to the earth at one point in its orbit (the PERIGEE) and farther from the earth at an opposite point (the APOGEE).

Polar orbits, geosynchronous orbits, and *low-altitude orbits* indicate the placement of the satellite's orbit around the earth. A satellite placed in a polar orbit is positioned so it passes almost directly over the North and South poles. As the earth rotates about the sun, the satellite orbit crosses the equator at different longitudes. This makes it possible for the satellite's instruments to gather information for the entire earth's surface. In addition, the satellite's position is such that it always crosses the equator at the same local time for each longitude. Weather satellites are one example of satellites that are placed in polar orbits.

When a satellite is placed in a high circular orbit, 22,235 miles (35,784 kilometers) above the earth at a velocity of 6,875 miles (11,064 kilometers) per hour, it is in a geosynchronous orbit. A satellite in this orbit travels around the earth's axis in exactly the same time, and same direction, as the earth rotates

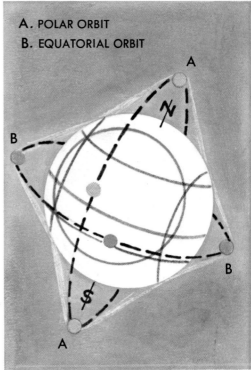

A. POLAR ORBIT
B. EQUATORIAL ORBIT

Figure 2—Example of an orbital system consisting of two orbits perpendicular to each other with four satellites in each orbit

about its axis. Because the satellite's orbit matches the earth's rotation, the satellite appears to remain in the same position over the earth. Communications satellites, which relay information between different points in space and on the earth, are often placed in geosynchronous orbits.

Many scientific research satellites are placed in low altitude orbits. These orbits tend to be in the highest layer of the earth's atmosphere, which is 300 miles (480 kilometers) above the earth. Because the orbit is so low, slight differences in velocity or direction cause the satellites to drift slowly off course.

TYPES OF SATELLITES

There are numerous types of satellites in orbit around the earth. One of the most important types is called *communication satellites.* These satellites relay radio signals around the earth for communications purposes. A communications satellite can relay several television programs or many thousands of phone calls at one time. A *ground station* on earth receives and transmits radio signals to the satellite. One important communications satellite is the Intelstat 4A, which sends signals between the continents.

Weather satellites provide information about weather patterns around the globe. Photographs from these satellites help scientists

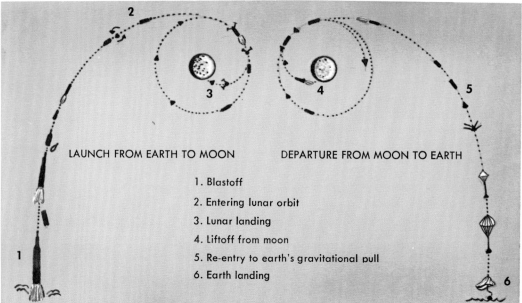

LAUNCH FROM EARTH TO MOON   DEPARTURE FROM MOON TO EARTH

1. Blastoff

2. Entering lunar orbit

3. Lunar landing

4. Liftoff from moon

5. Re-entry to earth's gravitational pull

6. Earth landing

Figure 3—Example of an orbital system consisting of a satellite cluster and rendezvous vehicles for contact with the earth's surface

locate storm systems, jet streams, fogs, snow, and cloud cover. Other instruments on the satellites measure temperature, air pressure and precipitation. The Geostationary Operational Environmental Satellite (GOES) is used by weather meteorologists to help forecast the weather.

Navigation satellites allow people to accurately determine their location on earth within 100 feet (30 meters). The radio signals sent out be these satellites are picked up by computerized receivers on aircraft, ships, and land vehicles. The first network of satellites used for navigation was called the Global Positioning System. A newer and larger system of navigational satellites is the NAVSTAR system.

Numerous *scientific research satellites* orbit the earth to observe the earth and its atmosphere or to study the sun, stars, and extragalactic objects. For example, the LANDSAT satellites have been used for making estimates of global wheat production, for forest and rangeland inventories, for mineral and oil exploration and geologic mapping, and for environmental monitoring and impact assessments. Another scientific satellite, the Gamma Ray Observatory (GRO) measures gamma rays that originate in outer space and maps their sources. The Hubble Space Telescope is also a scientific satellite.

Military satellites are usually communications, weather, research, and navigation satellites that are used for military purposes. Some military satellites, such as the Vela series, contain sensors that can detect nuclear explosions either on Earth or in space. Others can detect the launch of missiles, the movement of military equipment, and the locations of ships. Because these systems are used for military purposes, they are often called *spy satellites.* M.K.

SEE ALSO: SATELLITE, MAN-MADE; SPACE TRAVEL; SPACE VEHICLES; WEATHER FORECASTING

Orchard An orchard is a collection of fruit-bearing trees, especially APPLE, PEAR, PEACH, PLUM, CHERRY, APRICOT and QUINCE. Factors such as wind, light, nourishment, cold and heat influence the selection of a site for an orchard.

Yellow orchids

Purple orchids, most popular for corsages

Orchid (OHR-kid) The orchid is one of the most interesting and beautiful of all flowers. It has many different shapes and colors. All of the 12,000 known species resemble one another, but some are shaped more like a butterfly, some like a dove, and some like a lady's slipper. These exciting blooms, which come from the tropics and subtropics, may be colored white, yellow, purple, green, or brown.

There are two classes of orchids: those that take their food from the ground (*terrestrial*) and those that take their food from the air (*epiphytal*). The terrestrial orchids are found in moist, marshy places and in greenhouses. They are known as hardy, native varieties and have their resting period in the winter months. The epiphytal orchids attach themselves to the bark of trees and depend upon the moist, humid atmosphere for water. Sometimes these orchids are incorrectly called *parasites*. They merely cling to the trunks and limbs of trees and take nothing from the tree itself. In this group of orchids are the most beautiful and most valuable species.

The orchid flower is irregular. Two of the three petals are alike. The third one takes on many shapes, forming a *lip,* or *labellum.* This structural arrangement facilitates insect pollination. One pistil and one or two stamens are joined together. The roots are fibrous, tuberous or bulbous.

Orchids are propagated by division of the rhizome, stem cuttings and by seeds. The latter are very small and require very sterile germinating materials. One variety of climbing orchid produces a long pod that is dark brown when ripe. VANILLA is extracted from this plant. J. K. K.

Order see Animals, classification of; Plants, classification of

Ordovician see Geologic time table, Paleozoic Era

Ore Deposits of certain types of minerals can be found in places within the crust of the earth. Many of these deposits, such as metals and some other chemical compounds, are valuable to man. When rock contains a large quantity of these minerals, it is called an ore. The term ore is most often applied to metallic deposits, but it can also be used to refer to nonmetallic minerals.

Roasting, smelting, and electrolysis are commonly used in refining such metals as IRON, silver, gold, copper, aluminum, lead, and nickel. The presence of rich ore deposits adds greatly to a nation's wealth. Ore gives rise to industries that affect the lives of all people.

Ores are classified as two main kinds: *native elements* and *chemical compounds.* Native ore is found in nearly pure masses or bands interlayered but not chemically mixed with the enclosing rock. About 15 elements occur in nature, but only copper, silver, gold, platinum, carbon (graphite) and sulfur are found in dependable quantities. Thousands of other ores occur as compounds of the desired elements, commonly with oxygen, silicon, and sulfur. For example, iron ore is plentifully found as the oxide, HEMATITE, and zinc as the dark sulfide, *sphalerite.*

The chief factors in the formation of ore minerals are time, chemistry, and extreme heating, cooling, and pressure. Most of the iron ore deposits that we use today were formed long ago from an accumulation of iron-rich sediments in the deep ocean basins. E.M.N./P.P.S.

SEE ALSO: MINERALS, STEEL

Unloading Chilean lump iron ore

Oregano

Oregano (oh-RAY-gah-no) Oregano is an HERB that belongs to the mint family. Although some people call wild marjoram *origanum,* botanists say that origanum is a separate genus.

Oregano is a beautiful leafy perennial grown widely in the United States, Mexico, Italy, and Spain. It is used in powdered or dried-leaf form to season Mexican and Italian dishes, hot sauces, and bean dishes.

The herb plant may grow 3 feet (.9 meter) high in warm climates, has large clusters of pale, purplish-pink flowers, and oval, gray-green leaves. The flavor of oregano is more pungent than MARJORAM.

J.K.K.

SEE ALSO: MINT

Organ An organ is a many-celled part of an animal or plant made up of various tissues which work together to carry out some definite function. Examples are PLANT leaves and roots, and ANIMAL hearts and lungs.

SEE: ANATOMY, HISTOLOGY

Organic compounds Chemical compounds containing CARBON are defined as organic compounds. Most of the organic compounds also contain hydrogen, and a large number contain oxygen. Many contain nitrogen, sulfur, phosphorus, and other elements. The branch of chemistry now known as *organic chemistry* grew out of earlier studies of substances obtained from living organisms.

Natural organic compounds are found in plant and animal tissues. Familiar organic substances include sugar, fat, and petroleum.

Prehistoric peoples were familiar with organic compounds only in a practical way. In the production of wine, they fermented grape juice and produced alcohol. Soap was made from animal fats and olive oil. Dyes, such as indigo (a vegetable dye), alizarin (from a plant root), and Tyrian purple (from a Mediterranean species of mollusk) were used by the Romans and Greeks.

For many years people believed that organic compounds were obtainable only from living organisms. Thus the term "organic" indicated such compounds. But as chemical science developed in the early nineteenth century, many substances were made (*synthesized*) from nonliving chemicals. The first such organic synthesis was urea, made from CO_2 and ammonia. More recently, synthetic rubber has been produced. Today, thousands of organic compounds are made from nonliving sources.

While organic compounds are those containing carbon, inorganic compounds are those which do not contain carbon. Organic compounds outnumber inorganic compounds. Carbon atoms form *covalent bonds* with other atoms, linking them together in chains and rings of many different sizes and compositions and producing the practically unlimited number of organic compounds.

Organic compounds, with very few exceptions, are combustible. Inorganic salts, as a rule, do not burn. Organic compounds usually exist as gases, liquids, or low-boiling-point solids. Inorganic salts have very high melting points. Alcohols, sugars, and some metal-organic compounds dissolve in water, in this way resembling the many inorganic salts. But the many other organics are highly insoluble in water. Instead, they dissolve in other organic liquids like acetone or benzene. In theory, it is the covalent-bonded organics that dissolve in like substances having covalent bonds.

Familiar organic compounds are the hydrocarbons. Hydrocarbons occur plentifully in nature, particularly in PETROLEUM. NATURAL GAS, the gas used for cooking and heating in homes, is composed mostly of methane, the simplest of the hydrocarbons. Other hydrocarbons are ethane, propane, butane, and pentane.

Another group of organic compounds are the alcohols. Alcohols are used as solvents and starting materials for synthetic processes. Rubbing alcohol is the common

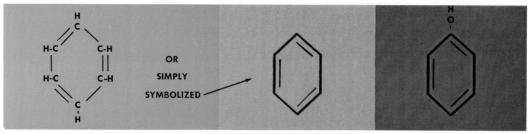

Benzene, C_6H_6, is the simplest of the benzene, or aromatic, group of organic compounds

A carbon benzene ring has a hexagonal formation

A benzene derived compound, phenol or carbolic acid

name for *isopropyl* alcohol. The ALCOHOL in beverages is made by fermentation of sugars. An enzyme in yeast, *zymase,* converts the sugar to ethyl alcohol and carbon dioxide. Another alcohol, ethylene glycol, is widely used as an ANTIFREEZE in automobile radiators.

ETHER may be prepared by adding sulfuric acid to ethyl alcohol. It is used as a general anesthetic or as a solvent.

The *aromatic,* or benzene-ring, compounds are another important and large group. Benzene has the formula C_6H_6 and is not arranged atomically like the carbon compounds mentioned before. Its six carbon atoms are linked in a closed chain. Between alternate atoms there is a double bond of two pairs of electrons. Some benzene-ring compounds are fragrant substances found in plants; for example, balsams, resins, and perfume oils and flavorings. Still other benzene-ring molecules are made in animal and human cells; for example, hemoglobin in the blood and several hormones such as thyroxin and adrenalin all contain complex ring molecules.

Inorganic chemistry is used in geology, metallurgy, and mineralogy because it deals with inorganic materials such as gases in the atmosphere, water, rocks, minerals, metals and their salts, nonmetals and their compounds (i.e. sulfuric acid.) Organic chemistry is applied in physiology, biochemistry, and in the science of producing synthetic materials. Through organic chemistry man has been able to improve upon nature by creating synthetic dyes, synthetic rubber, drugs and medicines, synthetic fibers, and many other useful compounds. Organic chemistry has given man a better understanding of the way in which living matter functions under normal conditions and of the causes of disease.　　　J. R. S.

SEE ALSO: CHEMISTRY, HYDROCARBONS

Organic rock Organic rock is rock formed from the remains of plants and animals. COAL, composed of plant material, and limestone, composed of shells and skeletons of sea creatures, are examples of organic rock.

SEE: PALEONTOLOGY, ROCKS

Organism An organism is any living thing, such as any form of animal or plant. It consists of dependent parts which work together to form common life for the whole.

Oriole (OHR-ee-uhl) Feathers of these songbirds vary from orange to yellow or green. Heads are usually black. Black wings are white barred. The center tail feathers are black, and those along the side of the tail match the body. All females are dull yellow or greenish-yellow in color.

Orioles belong to the blackbird family and are smaller than robins. They are found all over the United States except in parts of the south. Their cone-shaped, pointed bills are well adapted for insect feeding.

Nests are 8 to 10 inches (20 to 25 centimeters) long and carefully woven of grass, hair, and string. They are sacklike and hang from the tips of tree branches. Five or six white or bluish eggs with fine brown lines are laid. Both parents feed the young.　J.C.K.

Baltimore orioles weave a hanging nest

1223

Orion, the Hunter

Orion (oh-RYE-un) Orion is a large, bright CONSTELLATION which may be seen in winter. It is named after Orion, who was a great hunter. A row of three bright stars marks Orion's belt. Three fainter stars in a row represent a sword or a dagger hanging from his belt. Four more stars form a rectangle around the belt and sword. These mark his shoulders and knees.

Legends tell that Orion boasted he was the greatest hunter and no animal could kill him. A scorpion finally bit Orion and did kill him. The goddess Diana, a huntress, persuaded Jupiter to place Orion in the sky. Orion seems to be stalking the constellation, TAURUS, the bull. He is followed in his journey across the sky by Canis Major and Minor, his dogs. The scorpion is in the sky, too, but SCORPIUS is a summer constellation. This enemy of Orion is not visible when Orion is in the sky. Near the middle star in Orion's belt is a hazy cloud. This is the great Orion nebula, a gaseous cloud that reflects light from nearby stars.

BETELGEUSE, the bright red star on Orion's right shoulder, was supposed to be a ruby pin which held up his lion skin. Betelgeuse was the first star to have its diameter measured. Rigel, the bluish-white star diagonal to Betelgeuse, is pictured as the buckle on Orion's left shoe.   C. L. K.
SEE ALSO: NEBULA, STAR

Orion, dogs of   see Canis Major and Canis Minor

Ornithology see Bird

Ornithopter see Aviation

Orogeny (oh-REJ-ah-nee) Orogeny is the process of mountain formation. Most of the world's great mountain chains are located in narrow belts. All are characterized by highly folded *anticlines* and *synclines,* and *thrust faults* are common. Regional *metamorphism* and *igneous* intrusions of granite batholiths are usually present. This type of structure is called an *orogenic* system. The Appalachian and Rocky mountains are examples.

SEE ALSO: MOUNTAINS, PLATE TECTONICS

Chicago Natural History Museum
Eland, the largest antelope, is an oryx

Oryx The oryx is one of the largest members of the ANTELOPE family. Both buck and doe have long sharp horns. They inhabit open country in Africa. The best known are the *biesa,* the *fringe-eared* and the *desert* oryx.

Osage orange (OH-sayj) An osage orange tree looks as though it is loaded with green cannon balls. These green fruits, from 3 to 5 inches (7.6 to 12.7 centimeters) in diameter, are wrinkled and bumpy all over.

If the fruit or stem is cut, a bitter milky juice will flow. The branches have sharp thorns. Trees are sometimes planted close together for a hedge. The ROOTS are colored a brilliant orange. The Indians and early settlers at one time used these roots as a dye for their clothing and blankets.   V.V.N.

Oscillator An oscillator is an electric circuit which produces alternating voltage of required frequency. In RADIO transmitters, the electromagnetic waves produced by an oscillator serve as CARRIER WAVES. Audio oscillators vary frequency in test equipment and MUSICAL INSTRUMENTS.

Oscillatoria (ah-sill-uh-TOH-ree-uh) Oscillatoria is the growth sometimes found on the outside of flower pots. It is a plant without roots, stems, leaves, or flowers. It is a blue-green alga, the most simple form of plant. It reproduces by simple cell division.

Oscillatoria produces wide, narrow cells without organized nuclei. A blue pigment and CHLOROPHYLL are often present, though not localized in PLASTIDS. This alga is found on moist banks and cliffs or in the water. It has a jelly-like sheath, more visible in single-celled or colonial forms than in thread-like (filamentous) forms.

A species of oscillatoria is red and gives the Red Sea its name. P.G.B.
SEE ALSO: ALGAE; REPRODUCTION, ASEXUAL

Oscilloscope An oscilloscope is an electronic instrument which displays the image of an electrical signal on a fluorescent screen. The "heart" of the oscilloscope is a cathode-ray tube. Oscilloscopes are used to look at the waveform (shape) of an electric signal and to measure the strength and duration of very high frequency currents and voltages. When a serviceman fixes a television set, he looks at the waveform of the signal on the oscilloscope screen and compares it with a picture of what he should see.

An oscilloscope with *long persistence* has a screen coated with a special type of phosphor (the material which glows when bombarded with electrons) which will continue to glow at the spot the electrons have hit for a few minutes after the electrons have been removed.

It is sometimes necessary to compare two traces. This is most easily done using either

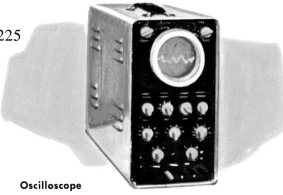
Oscilloscope

a dual-trace oscilloscope or a dual-beam oscilloscope. The *dual-trace* oscilloscope has a single electron beam which traces out one signal and then switches to trace out another signal. The long-persistence screen of this type of oscilloscope displays both traces at the same time.

Dual-beam oscilloscopes, on the other hand, use two electron beams. Each beam traces out a different signal. Both signals are displayed simultaneously on the screen. A long-persistence screen is not necessary in a dual-beam oscilloscope. M. R. L.
SEE ALSO: CATHODE RAY, CATHODE-RAY TUBE, ELECTRICITY, ELECTRONICS

Osier see Willow

Osler, Sir William (1849-1919) Sir William Osler was a Canadian physician who became famous because of the improvements he made in the teaching and practice of medicine. As the first chief-physician of Johns Hopkins Hospital in Maryland, he introduced the practice of having young doctors serve long terms as resident doctors in the hospital. When Johns Hopkins School of Medicine opened, he sent students into the wards to study at the bedsides of patients.

Because of his concern for training good physicians, Osler is primarily remembered as a great teacher. He also made specific studies of the blood and heart, malaria, cholera, and tuberculosis. He was often called "the great physician."

Born to pioneer missionary parents serving the Church of England in Tecumseh, Ontario, Canada, William lived eight years in the rugged poverty of the north woods. The family then moved to Dundas where William and his brothers and sisters could secure an education. Because of his boyish pranks, William was withdrawn from the local elementary school and sent to a boarding school in Barrie. Although he continued to be mischievous, he proved himself again and again to be an excellent scholar.

When he was sixteen, young Osler went to Weston, a preparatory school similar to Eton in England. It was there that he met the two men who were to determine the course of his life: Reverend William A. Johnson, founder and warden of the school, and Dr. James Bovell, an outstanding physician and teacher of medicine in Toronto. After receiving his medical degree from McGill University in Montreal, he traveled and worked in Europe and Canada. In 1888 he assumed the position of professor of the principles and practice of medicine at Johns Hopkins University. He also was named Physician-in-Chief at the new Johns Hopkins Hospital affiliated with the University. In 1911 he was knighted and made a baronet.

One book written by Osler, *The Principles and Practice of Medicine,* has been used for many years as a medical textbook. He spent the last two years of his life cataloging his priceless medical library which he bequeathed to McGill University.   D. H. J.

Osmium (AHZ-mee-um) An Englishman named Smithson Tennant discovered osmium, element number 76, in 1804. He named it *osmium* after a Greek word meaning "smell" because its compound with oxygen had a sharp and irritating odor. It is a hard grayish-white or bluish-white metal.

Osmium and a similar metal, IRIDIUM, form an alloy which is very hard. This alloy, *osmiridium,* is sometimes used for fountain pen points and phonograph needles.

Osmium is a dense element, a member of the PLATINUM group. It is more than ten per cent heavier than gold.

The oxide of osmium, osmium tetroxide or peroxide, OsO_4, is important in synthetic chemistry. The atomic weight of osmium is 190.2.   J. R. S.

SEE ALSO: ELEMENTS

Osmosis (ahs-MOH-siss) Osmosis is the movement of certain MOLECULES through a selective film (*semipermeable membrane*) toward the other side of the solution where the *concentration* of molecules is lower. In this process, an *osmotic pressure* is created against the membrane.

The constant motion of molecules causes them to spread (diffuse) on either side of a membrane. When large, slow-moving molecules—complex sugars, for example—are added to water on one side of a semipermeable membrane, the molecules start to mix through the solution. The smaller, fast-moving water molecules pass through the membrane, tending to dilute the sugar. Complex sugar molecules will bombard the membrane, be unable to pass through, and remain on the original side.

Many chemists and physicists include in osmosis the passage of any gas, liquid, or dissolved solid through a semipermeable membrane. Other scientists restrict the term to the passage of liquids and dissolved substances, such as food and minerals, through membrane. Most biologists, however, state that osmosis is the movement of water through a semipermeable membrane from where water is more concentrated to where it is less concentrated.

The classic experiment which shows osmosis uses parchment as the semipermeable membrane. The parchment allows water, but not molasses, to pass through.

The force by which water moves into the solutions is called osmotic pressure. Osmotic pressure depends upon the concen-

The classic experiment in osmosis uses a parchment membrane, thistle tube, molasses and water. The liquid rising in the tube is a solution of both fluids because diffusion occurs only one way—the water moves into the molasses

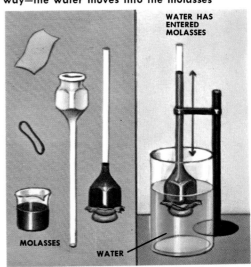

WATER HAS ENTERED MOLASSES

MOLASSES

WATER

✳ **THINGS TO DO**

WHICH MATERIALS WILL GO THROUGH A MEMBRANE?

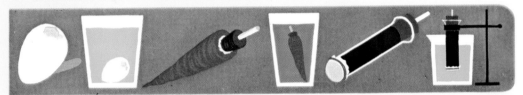

When two solutions are separated by a thin membrane, the stronger or more concentrated solution will pass through if the membrane is permeable to it. Set up several osmometers to determine which solutions go in which directions.

1 Carefully remove part of the shell at the large end of an egg. Do not break the membrane under the shell. Immerse the egg in a glass of water. What happens?

2 Hollow out the top end of a carrot or beet. Insert a one-holed cork into the hole and put melted wax around it to seal it closely to the root. Put a glass tube in the cork. Now place the carrot in colored water. What comes up the tube? Clear water or colored water?

3 Remove the bottom of a test tube by winding a wire around it and then holding this end over a flame. When the wire becomes hot it will break the end off the tube. Cover this open end with a cleaned piece of sausage casing. Fasten the membrane on tightly with a rubber band. Fill the tube with a molasses solution. Cap the tube with a cork and glass tube. Suspend the tube in a beaker of water from a ring stand. After several hours, observe the direction of liquid movement.

tration of water inside and outside the membrane and upon temperature. The greater the difference in concentrations and the higher the temperature, the greater the osmotic pressure. This pressure is frequently measured in pounds per square inch or millimeters of mercury. It helps make sap in plants rise.

Living cells have a membrane surrounding them through which osmosis can take place, but this membrane lets molecules pass into and out of the cell much more selectively than a simple semipermeable membrane can.　　　　J.K.L.

Osprey (AHS-pree) The osprey is a large bird, commonly known as the *fish hawk, bald buzzard,* or *fishing eagle.* The osprey is found throughout North America but prefers the South in the winter. The osprey dives feet first into the water and grips fish in its powerful talons. It is most often found along the coasts and near large lakes and rivers, but sometimes makes its home inland. It resembles the bald eagle but is smaller in size and has white underparts.

The osprey is about 2 feet (.6 meter) long, with a wing-spread of 4 feet (1.2 meters) from tip to tip. It is a rich brown color, and its tail is banded with brown and white. The upper parts of the head and neck are whitish, and the legs have a bluish cast. The voice of the osprey sounds like the peeping of baby chicks. Its nest looks like a bushel basket of sticks, built high in a dead tree, on a deserted building, or on the rocky ledge of a cliff.　　　　M.R.L.

SEE ALSO: BIRDS OF PREY

The osprey is a fish-eating hawk

Ossification (ahs-ih-fih-KAY-shun) Ossification is the formation of BONE; the changing of CONNECTIVE TISSUE or of CARTILAGE into bone through progressive changes in the cells making up the tissue. As large mammals, such as man, grow, the skull becomes ossified.

SEE: SKELETON

Ostrich (AWS-trich) Ostriches are the largest living birds. Males grow to 8 feet (2.4 meters) tall and weigh 300 pounds (136 kilograms). Females are smaller. They are flightless birds that can run at speeds up to 45 miles (72 kilometers) per hour or more.

Ostriches have fluffy black and white plumes on their bodies. Their necks are long. They are often in the company of GNUS and ZEBRAS. This is probably an association called *commensalism*. The ostrich is neither hurt nor aided by the association, but the other MAMMALS take advantage of the bird's keen vision.

The ostrich is the only bird that has two heavy toes (most have four). They protect themselves by kicking.

Males mate with two hens and build a family nest. Females lay twelve to eighteen very large, white eggs with pitted shells. Eggs are incubated for 42 days, during the day by females and during the night by the male. Young are covered with stiff down quills.

Fossil records show that ostriches came to the New World during the *Pleistocene* period. Those in South America evolved into *rheas*.

Ostriches thrive in captivity and have a life-span similar to that of humans.   J. C. K.

SEE ALSO: BIRDS, FLIGHTLESS

Chicago Natural History Museum
Sea otters of the Aleutian Islands

Otter (AHT-er) Otters are long, sleek, fur-bearing animals with long tails, short legs, and broad, webbed feet. They spend most of their time in water and are excellent swimmers, divers, and fishermen. These flesh-eating (*carnivorous*) mammals are closely related to WEASELS. There are two groups of otters, river otters and sea otters.

River otters grow to be about 4 feet (1.2 meters) long. Their grass-lined burrows may be found along the banks of streams and rivers. These playful animals love to slide down muddy or icy hills. They dive and swim in the water, catching fish with their sharp strong teeth. Otters also catch crayfish, snails, shellfish, frogs, and insects. River otters are active all year. Their bodies are covered with two layers of thick, water-repellent fur. The pale gray undercoat is short and soft, while the dark brown outercoat is long and stiff.

The otter's body is insulated by a layer of fat under the skin. In the early spring, two to three babies are born to each mother otter. The mother cares for them for several months.

Sea otters are larger and have shorter tails than river otters. They live in the vast beds of seaweed or KELP in the North Pacific. Their range is from the coast of North America north of Oregon to the Asian coast north of the Kurile Islands.

Only one baby sea otter is born at a time. The mother sea otter often sleeps on her back and carries her dependent baby on her chest. Sea otters seem to enjoy floating on their backs. They dive to great depths to catch crabs, mussels, snails, sea urchins, starfish and other marine life. They bring the food up to the surface, roll over to their backs, crack open their dinner and use their chests as tables to eat on.   D. J. A.

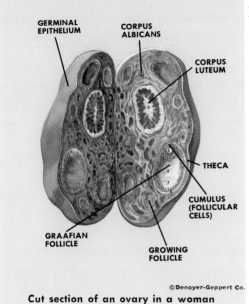

GERMINAL EPITHELIUM

CORPUS ALBICANS

CORPUS LUTEUM

THECA

CUMULUS (FOLLICULAR CELLS)

GRAAFIAN FOLLICLE

GROWING FOLLICLE

©Denoyer-Geppert Co.

Cut section of an ovary in a woman

Ovary (OH-vuh-ree) The ovary is the sex gland in a female. Within the ovary, germ or sex cells develop or mature into egg cells *(ova)* ready for fertilization.

There are two ovaries, each about 1½ inches (3.8 centimeters) long and ¾ inch (1.9 centimeters) wide in each female. When a baby girl is born, she has about 350,000 immature ova in the ovary, but only about 400 ever mature.

The maturing of ova is controlled by hormones secreted by the ovary and by the PITUITARY gland.

Germinal epithelium surrounds the ovary. Beneath it is the *cortex,* composed of fibrous and reticular connective tissue. It contains developing ova surrounded by follicle cells. A denser part of the cortex immediately under the epithelium is called the *tunica albuginea.*

The central part of the ovary is called the *medulla.* Developing ova are absent but there are smooth muscles, elastic fibers, and the branches of ovarian arteries and veins.

Germ cells mature by enlarging and going through the first division of meiosis. The second meiotic division takes place after the egg is in the oviduct and has been fertilized by a sperm. Follicle cells around the egg divide and secrete liquid until a large liquid-filled *Graafian follicle* is formed.

The mature egg is attached to one side of the Graafian follicle. When the follicle breaks, the egg passes into the oviduct. The empty follicle becomes the *corpus luteum* and secretes the hormone *progesterone.* If the egg has not been fertilized, the corpus luteum degenerates. J. C. K.

SEE ALSO: HISTOLOGY, MENSTRUATION, MITOSIS AND MEIOSIS, OVUM, REPRODUCTIVE SYSTEMS

Oven bird see Warbler

Overtones Musical sounds have three characteristics: pitch, loudness, and quality of tone. The tone quality, often called *timbre,* is determined by the number, strength, and pitch of all the separate tones comprising the one principal tone. This principal tone is called the *fundamental*—that is, a tone of a single frequency or pitch. The other weaker tones, not heard as separate tones, are called *overtones* (or *harmonics,* if they are multiples of the fundamental). A tone with a frequency twice the fundamental is called the first harmonic.

No musical instrument ever produces a pure tone, that is a tone of a single frequency. It actually produces a mixture of tones. A tuning fork, mounted on a resonating box, will usually produce a pure tone, with only the fundamental present. A pure tone is dull and colorless. The richness of the tones of musical instruments and of the human VOICE is due to overtones. The more overtones, the richer the tone quality.

If the same note, say middle C, is played on the violin, clarinet and piano, the pitch or fundamental frequency is the same. However, the quality of the tone differs in each case, and the listener with a little practice can distinguish the instruments producing the given notes. The difference in quality between instruments is due to the number and strength of the overtones produced at each frequency.

When a musical sound is made, the lowest and usually the strongest frequency in the mixture is the fundamental. It is the fundamental tone that seems to be heard.

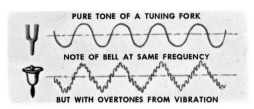

PURE TONE OF A TUNING FORK

NOTE OF BELL AT SAME FREQUENCY

BUT WITH OVERTONES FROM VIBRATION

The higher-pitched sounds are the over-tones. These are generally weaker vibra-tions of higher frequencies which affect the tones heard.

A string on a certain instrument may give, in addition to the fundamental of 200 vibrations per second, an intense overtone of 400 vibrations per second, with a mod-erate intensity; another of 1200 vibrations per second with less; and very faintly, others of 1600 and 2000 vibrations per second. A string on a different instrument may give the same fundamental, and the notes of 400 and 800 vibrations rather faintly, but may make the higher pitched overtones relatively loud. These two instruments thus differ in tone quality. Whenever the qualities of two tones of the same pitch are different, the overtones in the two are different either in pitch or loudness, or in both.   D. L. D.
SEE ALSO: MUSICAL INSTRUMENTS, SOUND

Oviparous (oh-VIPP-uh-ruhs) This term refers to animals that produce eggs that develop and hatch outside the female's body, even though they are fertilized within the body. The embryos are protected by jelly, shells, or mem-branes. The embryos are nurtured by yolk that is stored in the egg.
SEE ALSO: EGG, REPRODUCTIVE SYSTEMS

Ovoviviparous (oh-vo-vi-VIPP-uh-ruhs) This term refers to animals in which fertilized eggs develop inside the body of a female. The embryos are pro-tected and feed upon yolk stored in the egg. When mature, they are born either within the maternal body or im-mediately after the egg is expelled from the body.
SEE ALSO: GUPPY

Ovum (OH-vuhm) An ovum (egg) is the female reproductive cell produced

by the ovary. The maturation of eggs is called MEIOSIS and the release of them by the ovary is *ovulation*. Union of an egg and sperm, the male cell, is FER-TILIZATION.
SEE ALSO: EGGS; EMBRYOLOGY; GAMETE; OVARY; POLLINATION; REPRODUCTION, SEXUAL

Owl Owls are found all over the world. Most of them do their hunting at night and all are flesh eaters, prey-ing mostly on small rodents, such as mice. They have large heads, hooked beaks and talons and large eyes set in flat feathered disks. Their calls vary, depending on the species, from screeches and hoots to whistles and low moans.

Night-flying owls often prey over the same territory hawks cover during the day. They are well adapted for night hunting. Their eyes are ten to 100 times as sensitive to low light as man's and their ears, large slits in the sides of the head, enable them to hear the slightest rustling. Their flight feath-ers are fringed for silent attacks. They plunge at their prey and strike with their hooked talons. They differ from other birds of prey in that they may swallow prey whole and digest the meat, casting up indigestible items in the form of pellets.

There are about 133 species of owls, ranging from as small as a sparrow to large as a rooster. A few owls, such as the pygmy and hawk owl, hunt by day. They are soli-tary birds, some living far from civilization and others preferring human habitations where rodents are plentiful.

The smaller owls nest in holes in trees or on the ground and the large owls build nests. The female lays white, round eggs,

Some of the most common owls are the barn owl (left), horned owl (center), and screech owl (right)

Chicago Natural History Museum

Arctic musk ox

from one to 12 depending on the species. They hatch at intervals so the young vary in size.   E. R. B.

SEE ALSO: BIRDS OF PREY

Ox see Oxen

Oxen Oxen is a general term covering a group of hoofed animals belonging to the *bovine* family. They have some of the same body structures as cattle, sheep and goats. The only two wild oxen in North America are the bison and musk ox. The *kouprey* of Cambodia and the *gaur* (or *seladang*) of India are oxen of other countries.

Oxen generally have stocky bodies, cloven hoofs, large lateral horns, and a long tail. Their stomachs have four chambers, well adapted for digesting harsh grasses.

The *bison* is erroneously called BUFFALO in the United States. This wild ox is almost extinct in the wild state. Bison breed well in captivity. Their shaggy fur is brown to brownish black. The male may weigh up to 1,700 pounds (771 kilograms) while the female is somewhat smaller. Both sexes have horns that are never shed. The humplike shoulders are quite pronounced.

The *musk* ox is smaller than the bison and the domestic ox of other countries. It weighs under 500 pounds (227 kilograms). It gets its name from the strong musk odor it gives off when excited. Its shaggy hair is very long. As with bison, both the male and female musk oxen grow horns which are never shed; only new horny tissue is added annually. They are found roaming in groups around the Arctic region.

The *seladang* or *gaur* is a fast runner who spends its wild life in the forests of the Malayan Peninsula and India. It has horns measuring 2½ feet (.8 meter) long and stands about 6 feet (1.8 meters) high. The *Brahman ox (zebu)* has been brought to areas in southern United States from Africa. They are adapted to living and working in warm climates.   H.J.C.

SEE ALSO: ARTIODACTYLA, RUMINANT, YAK

1231   **Oxidation**

⁕ **THINGS TO DO**

WHAT ELEMENT IS NECESSARY FOR THE PROCESS OF OXIDATION?

1 Light a match and insert it into an empty glass jar. The match continues to burn because oxygen is present.
2 Now put a ball of steel wool into the jar. Sprinkle it well with water. Cover the jar and permit it to stand for several days.
3 Observe the change occurring to the steel strands. The steel wool is chemically combining with something in the jar to cause it to rust.
4 Remove the cover of the jar and immediately insert a lighted match. What happens to the flame? Steel wool cannot oxidize nor can fire burn without oxygen or a similar substance such as chlorine.

Oxidation (oks-i-DAY-shun) When the element oxygen acts chemically with another element to form a compound (an *oxide*), oxidation or combustion occurs. Oxidation may be rapid, as when wood burns, or slow, as when iron rusts. Substances other than oxygen also can cause oxidation. Atoms that capture electrons are oxidizers.

Chemists use the principle of *oxidation reduction* to explain whether a combining element's atoms either gain or lose electrons. A strong oxidizing agent takes electrons from another element in forming a new combination; a strong reducing agent gives electrons to capturing atoms.

It was once believed that when a substance burned, it lost weight and gave off a mysterious, weightless substance called *phlogiston*. This theory tried to explain that the saturation of air with phlogiston prevented the burning object from releasing any more to the air. Many prominent scientists, including Joseph Priestley, who was one of the first chemists to produce oxygen, believed in the phlogiston theory. For example, Priestley called the oxygen he produced "dephlogisticated air" because he believed that he had removed the phlogiston from the air.

Later (in 1777) Lavoisier proved that air consisted mainly of two substances, one which suffocated a mouse (nitrogen) and the other which supported combustion (oxygen). He showed that materials undergoing oxidation actually gained in weight, disproving the phlogiston theory. E. Y. K.

SEE ALSO: LAVOISIER, ANTOINE; OXIDE; OXYGEN; PRIESTLEY, JOSEPH

Oxidation number

When elements react chemically, they gain or lose electrons. This number of electrons is called the oxidation number. The oxidation number may be either positive or negative.

In the compound water (H_2O), oxygen has an oxidation number of -2, and hydrogen's oxidation number is $+1$. In water, each atom of oxygen takes two extra electrons. Each atom of hydrogen "donates" an electron to oxygen.

Many elements have several oxidation numbers. Nitrogen (N_2) has an oxidation number of $+1$ in nitrous oxide (N_2O), and $+4$ in nitrogen dioxide (NO_2). A.J.H.

Oxide

Oxygen exists alone or is chemically combined with other elements. An oxide is a compound usually made of two elements; one is oxygen and the other is usually a metal. Many useful mineral materials are oxides. Ordinary sand is silicon dioxide, SiO_2. Chinese white clay (kaolin) is aluminum oxide, and lime is calcium oxide.

Mineral oxides are used to obtain the metals with which they are combined in natural ores. The required removal of

Cryolite, with its low melting point, helps in reducing aluminum.

Photomicrograph by
National Teaching Aids, Inc.

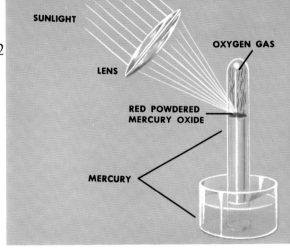

SUNLIGHT

LENS

OXYGEN GAS

RED POWDERED
MERCURY OXIDE

MERCURY

Lavoisier's experiment showed that a burned substance (mercuric oxide) can be made to reverse its action and release oxygen gas

oxygen, called *reduction,* is technically difficult. In reducing common hematite iron ore (which is Fe_2O_3), carbon monoxide from coked coal is the reducing agent:

$$Fe_2O_3 + 3CO \rightarrow 2\,Fe\;(iron) + 3CO_2.$$

Aluminum is reduced from its ore, bauxite, by a different method. First, the BAUXITE is treated with soda lye to obtain pure aluminum oxide; this is melted with cryolite ($Na_3Al\,F_6$) and reduced by electrolysis to yield pure molten aluminum.

Some of the nonmetallic oxides are very unstable. Sulfur dioxide, for example, is the choking gas formed when sulfur burns in oxygen or air. It will react with water to form sulfurous acid. E.Y.K.

SEE ALSO: ELECTROLYSIS, OXIDATION, REDUCTION

Oxyacetylene torch see Acetylene

Oxygen

(OK-si-jen) Oxygen is considered the most important element for life on this planet. Life can go on for a while without food or water, but not without oxygen. Oxygen is necessary also for fuels to burn.

Ancient philosophers did not know about oxygen as an element. They spoke of "something" in the air combining with fire. Zosimos, an Egyptian chemist, mentioned this as early as 250 A.D. Oxygen was not separated as a gas until 1772, when Karl Scheele of Sweden discovered it.

Independently, JOSEPH PRIESTLEY found oxygen but referred to the gas as "dephlogisticated air." He was surprised to

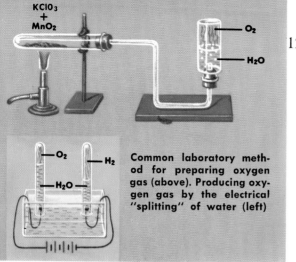

KClO₃ + MnO₂

O₂

H₂O

O₂

H₂

H₂O

Common laboratory method for preparing oxygen gas (above). Producing oxygen gas by the electrical "splitting" of water (left)

find that a candle burned more vigorously in the gas.

The importance of oxygen was realized neither by Scheele nor by Priestly but by the French chemist ANTOINE LAVOISIER. He identified oxygen as a material needed for combustion. Lavoisier's discoveries laid the foundation for modern chemistry.

About 20 per cent of the ATMOSPHERE is made up of oxygen. It is a colorless, odorless, and tasteless gas. Its density is .00143 grams per cubic centimeter. Oxygen (symbol O) has atomic number 8. Its atomic weight is 15.9994. Until 1961, it was the standard for the atomic weights of all elements: O = 16.000.

Oxygen is found in air as a *diatomic* molecule, O_2. It occurs in many compounds called OXIDES. The most plentiful oxide is plain sand (silicon dioxide, SiO_2). Large amounts of oxides are found in rocks, as iron or aluminum oxides, and as silicates ($-SiO_4$). Oxygen, next to silicon, is the most abundant element. About 50 per cent of the earth is made up of oxygen.

Oxygen also occurs in compounds called *peroxides,* which contain the peroxide ion. This ion is made of two oxygen atoms joined together by a *covalent bond.* The ion carries two negative charges. A peroxide commonly found in homes is hydrogen peroxide, H_2O_2. Hydrogen peroxide in water is used as a mild disinfectant and bleach. When hydrogen peroxide decomposes, it gives oxygen and water:

$$2H_2O_2 \rightarrow O_2 + 2H_2O$$

Oxygen is usually prepared in the scientific laboratory by the heating of potassium chlorate:

$$2KClO_3 \xrightarrow[\Delta]{MnO_2} 2KCl + 3O_2$$

Oxygen gas is liberated and collected by water replacement. Manganese dioxide is the catalyst in this reaction.

Oxygen is also produced by the electrolysis of water:

$$2H_2O \rightarrow 2H_2 + O_2$$

There are other methods of preparing oxygen. Commercially it is prepared by the liquefying of air. In the *Linde process* air is cooled until oxygen becomes a liquid at −183° C. (−297.4° F.). A few years ago gaseous oxygen was kept in tanks under pressure, but today liquid oxygen, which takes up less room, is kept in tanks as a space-saving measure.

Green plants produce oxygen during photosynthesis in daylight. Plants must use some oxygen from the air to carry on their own respiratory processes.

The ability of oxygen to support combustion, called *oxidation,* is its most significant property, and oxidation reactions always yield energy such as heat or light.

Tank oxygen is used in treating pneumonia and heart trouble. It is also used in flying, in submarines, in deep-sea diving, and in oxygen-acetylene torches.   E.Y.K.

SEE ALSO: COMBUSTION; ELEMENTS; LAVOISIER, ANTOINE; OXIDATION; PRIESTLEY, JOSEPH; SPONTANEOUS COMBUSTION

Oxygen tent An oxygen tent is a piece of medical equipment used for people with illnesses in which the body cannot get enough OXYGEN from air. The condition in which the body tissues are without oxygen is called *anoxia.*

An oxygen tent is a material (usually clear plastic) that can retain an oxygen-enriched air mixture around a patient. Even better than a tent (which is used for infants) is a mixture of oxygen and air passed through a tube strapped to the nostrils, where a more exact measure of the percentage of oxygen and the pressure of delivery can be determined.

These methods enable a patient to get more oxygen per inhalation than normally. A tank of liquefied oxygen serves as the oxygen supply. If respiration is weak, each inhalation must be rich in oxygen to compensate for the small air quantity inhaled. Various conditions require differing mixtures.   D.J.I./E.S.S.

J. W. Thompson

Japanese oyster

Oyster The oyster is a small sea animal enclosed in two hinged shells called *valves*. Oysters belong to a group of mollusks called *bivalves* (two-valves). Varieties are used for food, mother-of-pearl, and PEARL production. Oysters are found mainly in waters off sea coasts.

The full-grown oyster's shell is the size of a woman's hand, appearing grayish colored and irregularly pear-shaped. One valve is larger and cupped, holding the animal's soft body. The other is like a lid on a box. The inside of the valves is made smooth by a secretion of the oyster. This is "mother-of-pearl." Its smoothness protects the soft, naked animal. The valves open and close slightly, controlled by adductor muscles, located on either side of the body. Oysters breathe by GILLS and eat minute plants and animals in the water. To remove an oyster, one must force the shell open by cutting the strong muscles at the hinge with a sharp knife.

Oysters develop from eggs, one oyster producing hundreds of millions of eggs in a season. This large number of eggs is vital, for quantities are eaten by fish, which also devour the larvae (small swimming forms) which develop into adults. These swimmers travel about for two weeks until they anchor permanently. They continue to grow, arriving at full growth in three to four years.

Commercially, oyster "beds" are kept in favorable condition for oyster production and development. Since oysters live such perilous lives, "farmers" must do all they can to guard their investment by careful attention to oyster needs.   D. J. I.

SEE ALSO: MOLLUSCA

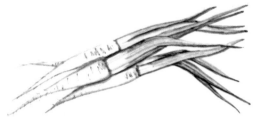

Salsify, with its oyster-flavored root

Oyster plant The oyster plant has narrow leaves and large yellow or purple flowers. There are several varieties which grow wild in Europe. The *salsify*, or purple goatsbeard, is grown in the United States for its edible, oyster-flavored root.

Ozone (OH-zohn) Ozone is an uncommon form of OXYGEN. It can be formed by passing an electrical discharge through oxygen. Only traces of it are found in the lower air. In the upper ATMOSPHERE, it occurs in greater concentrations. It is the only gas of the atmosphere that has an odor. The ozone molecule is made up of three atoms of oxygen (O_3) rather than the normal two atoms (O_2). The *ozone layer* of the atmosphere is normally concentrated at altitudes between 10 and 20 miles (16 and 32 kilometers).

Ozone would be poisonous to humans if it were concentrated near earth's surface. At high altitudes, however, it is essential to life. It absorbs almost all of the sun's ultraviolet rays that would otherwise destroy all exposed bacteria, stunt green plants, and severely burn animal tissue.

In the late 1970s, scientists discovered a hole in the earth's ozone layer over Antarctica. A smaller hole was discovered developing over the arctic region as well. Caused by gases called CFCs used in spray cans, refrigeration systems, and plastic packaging, damage to the ozone layer may soon threaten life on earth. In October 1992, the World Meteorological Organization reported that the Antarctic hole had reached a record size, covering an area three times the size of the continental United States.   H.S.G./J.H.

Ozonosphere see Atmosphere

Pacemaker see Heart

Pachyderm A pachyderm is a thick-skinned, hoofed animal such as an ELEPHANT, RHINOCEROS, or HIPPOPOTAMUS. Cud-chewing animals (ruminants), such as cattle and goats, are also hoofed but are not pachyderms.

The pachyderm group is a popular group rather than a scientific one. Taxonomically most pachyderms are not even classified in the same order of mammals and are not closely related. For instance, the hippopotamuses are more closely related to cattle than to elephants, and yet cattle are not pachyderms. J. C. K.

Paddlefish The paddlefish, or duckbill, is a freshwater fish found in the Mississippi River and its branches. It is scaleless, and sometimes reaches a length of 6 feet (1.8 meters) and a weight of 150 pounds (68 kilograms). It is related to the sturgeon, and its eggs are often mixed with eggs of the sturgeon for caviar. Another species of paddlefish is found in China.

Pahoéhoé lava Pahoéhoé lava is a very smooth or ropey type of basalt

Paddlefish
Chicago Natural History Museum

lava. It is a fluid lava that resembles thick syrup. It got its name in Hawaii, where it is common.

Pahoéhoé lava results from eruptions of basaltic volcanoes, those producing the hottest, most fluid lavas. This type of lava tends to stream down the volcanic cones and congeals to form tongues only 3 feet (1 meter) thick. The ropey appearance occurs as the lava cools but is still moving. Pahoéhoé lava is common to volcanic structures in Hawaii and Iceland. The fluid nature of Pahoéhoé lava is due to its low silica content and low *viscosity*. P.P.S.

Pain Pain may be defined as suffering or distress in the body. Many animals, including people, can feel pain. Pain is one of man's oldest enemies, and man tries hard to avoid pain whenever possible. Pain is also a great friend of man, however, because it is the body's way of reporting DISEASE, INFECTION, or injury of certain body parts. Some people cannot feel pain because their "pain nerves" do not function properly. Such a person might burn himself accidentally and not realize it.

Pain is detected by thin, bare, finely branching nerve endings in the skin and internal organs of the body. These nerves are like tiny electric wires. Their impulses run up the SPINAL CORD to the brain where they are perceived as pain. Pain can be of many types: dull and constant, sharp and shooting, rhythmical and cramping, moderate or severe. Pain is a very personalized sensation. No one can really know the intensity of pain felt by another person. Doctors have special drugs, particularly NARCOTICS, for the relief of intense pain. Some *chronic* pains can be relieved by cutting nerves in the spinal cord so the impulses do not travel to the brain. New techniques such as *acupuncture* can sometimes relieve chronic pain, for reasons not yet known. Some researchers think that the human brain can produce powerful natural pain relievers, called *endorphins,* and that they are built up because of stimulation of nerves by acupuncture needles. B.M.H.
SEE ALSO: NERVE CELL

✳ **THINGS TO DO**

CAN YOU MAKE A BLACK PAINT?

1   For making homemade black paint you need carbon or lampblack, turpentine, and linseed oil.
2   Lampblack can be obtained by holding a pyrex dish or bottle over a candle flame until the carbon forms on it. Scrap the film of black into a small amount of linseed oil.
3   Mix these materials thoroughly. Add a few drops of turpentine to make the paint thin enough to spread on a surface. The result will be a flat permanent paint. Shiny enamel paint is obtained by adding a few drops of varnish to the flat mixture.

Paint Paint is used to color and protect a surface. The color is due to pigment, a dry, colored powder that is mixed with a liquid. This liquid is called the *vehicle.* After paint stands in a container for a long time, the pigment will settle to the bottom and the vehicle, usually clear, can be seen at the top.

Paints differ according to the vehicle used. *Water paints* depend upon the caking action of the pigment powder to adhere to the painted surface. Glue or paste may be added to improve adhesion, as is the case in calcimine, casein paints, and whitewash. Latex paint uses water to separate particles of latex rubber. As the water evaporates, particles stick together and to the painted surface. This paint can be washed out of rollers and brushes with soap and water before it dries. After the paint dries, stronger solvents are required for cleaning.

Solvent base paints use a chemical solvent to dissolve a solid material. *Lacquer* is the combination of a resin produced by certain trees and the solvent toluene. Shellac is the shell of the lac insect dissolved in alcohol.

Greater durability and protection is obtained from *oil paints.* Linseed oil, obtained from the seed of the flax plant, is commonly used as the vehicle. It reacts with the oxygen in the air to form a tough, waterproof film that seals and protects the surface and holds the pigment particles together. Most oil paints are too thick to apply easily with a brush or sprayer. A thinner, such as turpentine or *oleum,* makes the paint easier to apply and also speeds drying.

Enamels use varnish as the vehicle. Varnish is highly resistant to scratching. This is why it is used uncolored on wood floors. The varnish in enamels provides a shiny surface that looks like porcelain enamel. Enamel lasts longer than most other paints.   M. W. K.
SEE ALSO: PIGMENT, VARNISH

Painted cup see Wild flowers

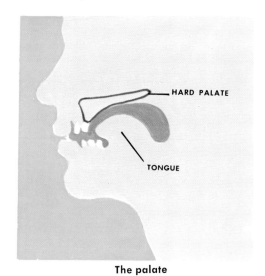

HARD PALATE

TONGUE

The palate

Palate The palate is the roof of the mouth. The front part, called the *hard palate,* is bony and hard; and the back portion, called the *soft palate,* is muscular and soft. Both are covered with MUCOUS MEMBRANE. They separate the mouth and the nasal cavity.

Paleolithic see Stone Age

Paleontologists may first make ground surveys of an area which is likely to hold fossils. Then, when a fossil is found it must be removed from the ground very carefully. The rock around it may be useful in dating the specimen

Paleontology (pay-lee-uhn-TAHL-uh-jee) Paleontology is the science that deals with *fossils*. Fossils are the remains of plant and animal life from thousands of years ago. Paleontology is often considered to cover just fossil animals, but a better division of this science is to use *paleozoology* for the study of fossil animals and *paleobotany* for the study of fossil plants. "Paleo" is from the Greek word *palaios,* meaning "ancient."

Fossils are useful as evidence of evolution. A collection of them may show the changes that a certain kind of animal has gone through. Fossil bones of early man found all over the world show the story of the changes from ape to modern man. These changes took almost two million years. As a general rule, paleontology usually does not deal with things less than 10,000 years old.

Discoveries in paleontology occur every year, sometimes accidentally. In November 1992, fossil remains of a camel, a mastodon, and other MAMMALIA were found by highway construction workers in California.

In January 1993, a University of Chicago paleontologist made an even more exciting announcement. Near the Andes mountains in Argentina, Chicago scientists discovered fossilized bones of the oldest DINOSAUR yet found. The new species, named Eoraptor, stood only three feet (less than one meter) tall and ate meat. It lived 225 million years ago.

Paleontology is closely connected to GEOLOGY, the study of the earth's crust, including the sediment at the bottom of the ocean. Impressions such as footprints of past animals are often found in rocks. Though a fossil is rock, when the animal left an impression the surface was probably moist sand or clay. Physical changes on the earth's surface determine whether or not remains will be preserved as fossils.

Fossils tell the geologist much about the earth. He may want to know how old a rock is. If the rock contains fossils of animals that he knows lived only about 100,000 years ago, he can be fairly sure that the rock is about 100,000 years old. Such fossils are called *index* fossils.

HISTORY OF PALEONTOLOGY

The first notice and scientific interpretation of fossils was recorded by the Greek Xenophanes in 600 B.C. He observed fossils of mollusks inland, away from the sea, and thought that the sea had once covered that area. In Egypt one hundred years later, Herodotus observed shells in the desert and tried to interpret them.

Not until the beginning of the scientific renaissance in Europe, about 1400 A.D., did fossils again come to be considered as evidence of changes on Earth. Leonardo da Vinci was the first expert since the classical times of ancient Greece to recognize fossils without superstition. About the same time, they were mentioned in a scientific book by the geologist Agricola.

Modern paleontology started about 1800 from the work of two men—BARON GEORGES CUVIER and William Smith. Smith found that in different layers (strata) of rock, different

1237

When the fossil is recovered, it may be gently scraped or bathed in acid and fixed so it can be studied or displayed without damaging or destroying it

fossils were found. His work started *stratigraphical* geology and, in large part, had a basis in the use of index fossils. Cuvier, however, studied fossils in the same way that zoologists and anatomists study living things. He tried to interpret the habits and environments of past animals from their fossil structures. The work of these two men brought about the first division of general paleontology into separate areas.

FIELDS OF PALEONTOLOGY

Paleobiochemistry: A very specialized field of paleontology is paleobiochemistry. This area of study is confined to studying fossils for remnants of organic compounds. Workers in this area of biochemistry have been able to identify animo acids in fossils up to 360,000,000 years old. These scientists know that the older the fossils are, the fewer amino acids remain.

Paleobotany: The study of fossil plants and vegetation has become very important for a knowledge of environmental conditions in the geologic past. Paleobotany has been, and is, vital to a clear scientific description of the evolution of plant life on earth.

Evidence of the *angiosperms* (flowering plants which now dominate the earth) are found only in deposits made after the middle of the Mesozoic Era. The *thallophytes* (algae and seaweeds), on the other hand, have existed for more than 500 million years. There are eleven large groups of plants which are known only in fossil form, as the dinosaurs are known. The most dramatic plant fossils are the giant logs of petrified wood.

Collecting plant fossils is more difficult than collecting animal fossils because of the delicate plant structures that are so easily destroyed or carried away by water. Leaf deposits are often found in thin layers of fine sediment. Usually only impressions will be found because moisture caused the leaf to decay. Some fragments, though, will have been *carbonized* and are more easily preserved.

Paleoclimatology: Paleoclimatology is part of paleogeography. It deals with winds, precipitation, weather, and climate zones of past geologic ages. The study is based on rocks and organic remains.

Paleoecology: The ecology of fossil life is a more difficult study than the ECOLOGY of living things. Because of the vast geologic changes, the science has to be based on inferences. Its basic assumption is that plants and animals in the far past formed an interrelated and balanced society much as they do today. Most data are in the area of marine biology, because more fossils are found in marine sediment than are found on land or in fresh water.

Paleogeography is primarily concerned with the geography of the past and deals with fossils only in describing areas.

There are several other terms that fall into the general area of paleontology. *Paleoethnology* is the study of races, cultures, and specializations of prehistoric man. *Paleontography* is the straight physical description of fossils.

COLLECTING FOSSILS

Searching for fossils can be an interesting hobby or career. They may be found accidentally, but it is necessary to have some general knowledge of geology and zoology to understand what they are. On discovering fossils, it is important for the amateur to note carefully the kind and location of rocks they were found in. The fossil can sometimes be identified with the help of the rock type. If the rock cannot be easily identified, the amateur should take careful note of the location so that an expert can identify it.

An experienced paleontologist may be able to compare the fossil find with other fossils and with living things. For this, a knowledge of biology is vital.   J.F.B./J.H.

SEE ALSO: BALANCE OF NATURE, CLIMATE, EARTH, ECOSYSTEM, EVOLUTION OF MAN, FOSSILS, GEOLOGIC TIME TABLE, PETRIFACTION, ROCKS, SOIL TYPES, TRILOBITE

Corals of the middle Cambrian life

Marine invertebrates of the late Ordovician

Paleozoic Era (pay-lee-uh-ZOH-ick) The period of ancient life called the Paleozoic Era began about 600 million years ago and came to an end about 200 million years ago. Great changes in life took place throughout this era.

During this 400 million years many changes occurred, with a progression from the Age of Invertebrates to the Age of Fishes and the Age of Amphibians. During this era came the first vertebrates, land animals, insects, plants, forests, and seed-bearing plants.

The Paleozoic Era also saw a variety of climates. During long periods of warm dry temperatures, great deposits of salt were formed. There were also periods of warm humid climate in which vast coal-forming swamps came into existence. There were periods of very cold climate when huge glaciers covered the earth.

There were seven recognized periods that made up the Paleozoic Era. They are named after places where rocks of the period were first studied. Listed in order of occurrence they are: Cambrian, Ordovician, Silurian, Devonian, Mississippian, Pennsylvanian, and Permian. European writers refer to the Mississippian and Pennsylvanian periods together as the Carboniferous, or coal-forming, Period. The Appalachian revolution took place during the Paleozoic Era and resulted in the creation of the Appalachian Mountains near the close of the era.

There were many changes geographically during this period of ancient history. Large inland seas were formed when rising ocean waters flooded interior areas of North America. At other times uplifting occurred, the seas receded, and mountains may have been formed. These inland seas of the seven periods of the Paleozoic Era differed considerably in extent and location. There was no regular pattern or sequence to their origin and disappearance. Some existed for very long periods of time, while others were of shorter duration. Some formed at the start of periods, others in the middle or at the end. The three largest inland seas occupied broad shallow depressions known as the Appalachian Trough, the Cordilleran Trough, and the Ouachita Trough. The Appalachian Trough was located roughly where the Appalachian Mountain chain is today. The Cordilleran Trough occupied the Rocky Mountain area of today. The Ouachita Trough stretched from across Oklahoma to Texas and New Mexico.

This was an era of many changes. There were many beginnings, evolutional processes, and endings during the era known as the Paleozoic Era. V.V.N.

SEE ALSO: GEOLOGIC TIME TABLE

Palladium (puh-LAY-dee-um) Palladium is a metallic element. It has a bright silvery luster. This rare, grayish element is less dense, a little harder, and more easily oxidized, than platinum. It is found in platinum, nickel and copper ores.

Pure palladium is used in the manufacture of mirrors and watch springs. It is also used in alloys with gold, platinum, and silver. These alloys are used for jewelry, dental equipment, picture frames, pocketbook trim, and scientific instruments.

Palladium (symbol Pd) has atomic number 46. It has an atomic weight of 106.4. It was discovered in 1804 by William Wollaston. M.R.L.

SEE ALSO: ALLOY, ATOM, ELEMENTS

From left to right: royal palm of Africa, flower of the date, palmetto—a small tropical American palm, and Travelers palm of Africa

Palm There are about 2000 kinds of plants in the palm family. They range from small house plants to trees up to 100 feet (30.5 meters) tall. They are found in tropical areas. The trunk usually has no branches. The small flowers are either male or female blooms. The fruit is a drupe or berry.

Palms belong in the *monocotyledon* subclass of angiosperms. The leaves may be pinnately compound as in the DATE palm, or palmately compound as in the fan palm. The stem may be spiny, smooth, or covered with stumps of old leaves.

Economically, palms are important to man. The COCONUT palm's rating is near the top. The natives have found over 800 uses for the *Palmyra palm. Royal palms* withstand strong winds and are popular ornamental trees in Florida. The *American oil palm* produces 2000 nuts annually for 50 years. The *cohune palms* of South America also yield an oil.

The pith of certain palms gives *sago* starch. The buds of *cabbage palms* are eaten. Leaves of the *hat palm* are dried, bleached and woven into hats. The *tagua palm* seed furnishes a vegetable ivory for buttons and dice. The epidermis of the *raffia palm* leaf is woven into baskets. Wax from *carnauba palm* leaves is used in varnish. H. J. C.

SEE ALSO: MONOCOTYLEDON; PLANTS, TROPICAL; RAFFIA

Palmate venation see Leaves

Palsy see Paralysis

Pampas see South America

Panama Canal see South America

Pancreas (PAN-kree-uhs) The pancreas is a gland shaped rather like a fish. It is found in the abdomens of animals with backbones. The pancreas plays a double role in the body. It produces *enzymes* needed to digest all kinds of food. Small sections of the pancreas, called the *islands* (or *islets*) of *Langerhans,* produce a *hormone* that enables the body to use sugar.

The human pancreas is about 6 to 9 inches (15.2 to 22.9 centimeters) long and 1½ inches (3.8 centimeters) wide. It lies behind the stomach and a little below it. The right end of the pancreas is folded forward around a group of blood vessels. This hook-like piece is called the *head.* The digestive juice is collected in a duct that leads from the pancreas to the duodenum.

INSULIN is the hormone produced by tissues in the pancreas. Unlike the digestive juices, it is a ductless (*endocrine*) secretion and enters the body through the blood vessels. It is called *insulin* from the Latin word *insula,* meaning *island,* because it is secreted by the islands of Langerhans. If they do not make enough of it, the body cannot burn sugar. This condition is called *diabetes mellitus.* D. A. B.

SEE ALSO: ENDOCRINE GLANDS

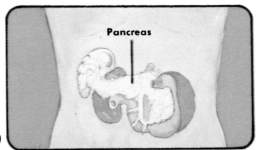

Pancreas

Giant panda

Pansies

Panda Pandas look like bears or cats, but they belong to the raccoon family. They are found only in the mountains of western Tibet. All other members of the raccoon family live in America. There are two pandas. The giant panda has a bearlike tail; the lesser panda has a striped raccoon-like tail. The teeth of both kinds are similar to those of meat eaters, although they eat bamboo shoots primarily.

The lesser panda is about the size of a house cat. It strikes with its front paws like a bear and climbs like one. Its claws are partly retractile, like a cat's. The body is covered with long, thick, rusty-colored fur. The face is white with dark stripes from the eyes to the corners of the mouth.

The giant panda, one of the rarest of large mammals, is the size of a bear. It can climb, but it usually lopes along on flat feet. On the toes of the front feet are pads for holding food. Molars are wide and flat for crushing bamboo. Although giant pandas are small at birth, they weigh 60 pounds (27.2 kilograms) after a year. They reach full growth in about five years and can weigh 300 pounds (136 kilograms). J.C.K.

Pandanus Pandanus is a large family of house plants, shrubs, or trees. The trees may be over 50 feet (15.2 meters) high. They are called *screw pine* because of the spiral or screwlike pattern of the LEAVES on the stem.

Many species in this family develop prop roots. These are roots that raise above the soil. Both the FLOWER and the FRUIT form a cluster. The fruit looks like a pine cone. Each flower is unisexual. There may be one or many pistils or many stamens, but there are no sepals and petals.

The name pandanus is given to a whole group of flowering plants of the family Pandanaceae. H.J.C.

Pansy The pansy is probably one of the oldest cultivated plants. It is related to the VIOLET. For at least 400 years, the pansy, which is native to Europe, has taken to all cool, temperate climates of the civilized world.

The pansy is a low-growing plant, seldom more than six inches tall. It has heart-shaped leaves and large, irregular flowers that look like human faces. The blossoms may be purple, white, blue, yellow, brown or a mixture of these colors.

Pansies should be grown in partial shade and given plenty of moisture. When the air becomes dry during the hot summer months, the pansy plant is apt to fail even though it may be in the shade. Some pansies are annuals; some are perennials. J. K. K.

Panther see Cat family

Papaya (puh-PAH-yuh) Papayas are herbs that are sometimes called *paw-paw trees.* Papayas grow in tropical America. They are about 18 feet (5.5 meters) tall and look like palm trees. They have a cluster of huge leaves on top. Papaya fruits ripen in midwinter or early spring. They taste somewhat like muskmelons. They are yellow or orange and weigh as much as 20 pounds (9 kilograms). Papaya fruits have a strong odor.

The unripe fruit is cooked like squash. The milky juice and black seeds inside the fruit are rich in papain. *Papain* is used in medicine and as a meat tenderizer. Papayas need sunshine, well-drained, rich loam, and frequent cultivation. M. R. L.

Papaya tree and fruit

The huge rolls of paper will be used on large printing presses   Westvaco

Paper The discovery of paper contributed greatly to civilization. Writings have been traced back thousands of years to a time when signs and words were made on bark, bricks, skins, and other surfaces.

If man had observed nature and watched paper-making wasps use wood pulp, he might have made paper earlier. The wasps chew the pulp and spread it in thin layers to form the walls of their nests.

Today there are about 5,000 different types of paper with almost as many uses. The consumption of paper is enormous. Over 400 pounds (181 kilograms) per person are used in a single year.

Paper is made from CELLULOSE or vegetable fibers. In the early days of paper-making, rags were the chief source of fiber for paper. Today the chief source of cellulose for paper is wood. When the forests were abundant, preferred woods were selected. Today, many kinds of wood are used for pulp, including pine, spruce, hemlock, fir, poplar, beech, birch, maple, and aspen.

Many successful experiments have been made to produce paper from fibrous materials other than wood. But while the supply of wood lasts, it seems to be the easiest and most economical pulp material. Paper has been made from hemp, turf, moss, potato skins, tobacco waste, coconut husks, bean stalks, cabbage leaves, bamboo, and many other vegetable materials. The important considerations for pulp material are the need for long enough fibers to make strong paper, the ease of changing the material to fiber form and eliminating impurities, availability of large supplies of low cost material, and economical means of getting the pulp materials to the mills.

If a sheet of medium-weight paper is held up to a good light, the paper can be seen to be made up of small fibers matted together. The logs that arrive at a pulp mill have to be reduced to these small fibers. One of the methods used is mechanical, the others are chemical. In the mechanical, or ground-wood method, pulp is produced by grinding the wood with grindstones under water. The chemical process takes wood chips that have come through a chipping machine, combines them in a digester, an enormous pressure cooker, with chemicals and cooks them to pulp. Different chemicals are used depending on the kind of wood used and the kind and grade of paper desired. There are sulfite (acid), sulfate (alkaline), and soda processes used in chemical methods.

The pulp, which is about 95 per cent water, is usually bleached and then goes to the paper machine. The pulp is spread onto a screen-like bed, which moves forward as it drains off some of the water and jostles from side to side to mat the fibers. The pulp is rolled between felt rollers to absorb moisture and pressed and dried as it goes through a series of rollers. The continuous sheet emerges and is wound in large rolls as finished paper to be used in manufacturing paper products.   C. L. K.

SEE ALSO: FOREST PRODUCTS, PAPYRUS, PRINTING

Red pepper, or capsicum, plant

Paprika Paprika is a spice made by grinding the dried pod of the red pepper, or *capsicum,* plant. It is a reddish powder, sweeter in taste than CAYENNE or chili pepper. It is often used for decorating foods such as mashed potatoes or creamed chicken.

The capsicum plant belongs to the NIGHTSHADE family and is not related to the *Piper nigrum* plant from which black and white pepper are made. The capsicum plant is an annual shrub bearing small white flowers and reddish oblong fruit which stands upright on the branch. These pods are called *pimiento.* J. M. C.

SEE ALSO: PEPPER, SPICE

Papyrus (puh-PY-ruhss) Papyrus is a tall reed-like plant that lives in wet places. It was used by the ancient Egyptians, Greeks, and Romans to make a writing material like paper. The word "paper" comes from the word "papyrus."

The Greeks peeled thin strips from the papyrus stem, pasted or pounded the strips together, smoothed them with shells, and rolled the sheets into scrolls.

Papyrus was also used for making boats, rope, sailcloth, and mats. The roots were used for fuel and the flowers for decorating the shrines of gods. Today, the plant is quite rare and usually found only as decoration in water gardens. J. M. C.

SEE ALSO: PAPER

Papyrus plant

Paracelsus

Paracelsus, Philippus Aureolus (pair-uh-SELL-suss) (1490-1541) Paracelsus was a Swiss physician and alchemist. An alchemist was a medieval chemist who attempted to prolong life indefinitely, to discover a universal cure for diseases, and to change common metals into gold. As a physician, Paracelsus preceded SIR JOSEPH LISTER in maintaining "All that is necessary [to heal wounds] is to prevent infection in wound diseases."

Paracelsus was born near Einsiedeln, Switzerland. He received his early education from his father who was a physician and chemist. He studied at the University of Basel, but left without getting a degree. Traveling to the mines in Tyrol, he studied the mechanical problems of mining, composition of minerals, and diseases of miners.

When he returned to lecture at the University of Basel in 1526, Paracelsus was met by intense opposition. His books in which he set forth his theories and methods of treating disease were burned by his enemies before he could begin his series of lectures.

He also lectured in German instead of Latin, the language of scholars, which was an inexcusable breach of their scholarship.

His opponents declared that his ideas had serious defects and that he did not have a degree. Finally, feeling became so heated that Paracelsus was forced to flee Basel. He wandered from place to place until 1541 when Archbishop Ernst invited him to live in Salzburg and offered him protection. However, his security lasted only a short time, for on September 24 of that same year Paracelsus met a tragic and brutal death at the hands of his enemies when he was thrown down a steep incline. D. H. J.

SEE ALSO: ALCHEMY, MEDICINE

WHY DOES A PARACHUTE MAKE AN OBJECT DESCEND SLOWLY?

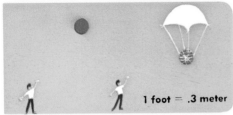

1 foot = .3 meter

1 Go outside in an open area and throw a ball as high as you can. Observe how fast the ball returns to the ground.
2 Now tie a network of strings around the ball. Attach four long strings to four sides of the ball by tying them to the net. Tie the other ends of the strings to the corners of a two-foot square of cloth. Wrap the lines and parachute around the ball.
3 Again throw the ball as high as possible. Does the ball descend at the same rate of speed? Any falling body must push aside the resisting air. Since the parachute encounters a much greater area of air, it falls more slowly.

Parachute The parachute was invented to allow men to escape from BALLOONS from above the earth. Today it is also used for dropping cargo to places difficult to reach in other ways. Fast planes may use parachutes to help in stopping or braking while landing. Sport parachuting, called sky-diving, is popular today.

An open parachute looks like a huge stickless umbrella. Closed or folded into a bundle, it looks like the pack of an overnight camper.

Any falling object has two main forces acting on it: the pull of *gravity* and the *resistance of the air*. GRAVITY, the stronger force, accelerates a man in free fall to about 120 miles (193 kilometers) per hour when at lower altitudes. The broad-surfaced open parachute increases the air resistance, assuring a slower, safer rate of descent.

Once away from the aircraft, the falling parachutist pulls the *ripcord*, releasing a small *pilot chute* about 3 feet (.9 meter) in

DO OBJECTS OF THE SAME WEIGHT FALL AT THE SAME SPEED?

1 You will need two sheets of ordinary typewriting paper approximately the same in size and weight for this experiment. Leave one as it is; wad the other tightly into a ball.
2 Stand on a chair for added height. Stretch arms and hands straight out in front, palms up. On one palm is the paper ball, on the other the flat sheet of paper. Quickly pull your hands away, letting both objects fall to the floor. Try timing the two descents with a stop watch.
3 What fact about the papers would account for the results you obtained?

E.M.N.

diameter. This catches the airstream and pulls out the larger *main chute* or *canopy* which may be 24 feet (7.3 meters) in diameter. Spaced evenly around the canopy's edges are about 36 long ropes or *shrouds*, connected to the harness worn by the parachutist. A hole or vent in the top of the canopy stabilizes the canopy's descent by letting some air escape. Fast modern aircraft have ejection seats so that the pilot can, by exploding a gunpowder device, be thrown clear of his aircraft and then open his chute to come down safely.

The parachutes of today are made of NYLON which has great strength and flexibility.

The parachute idea has long intrigued men. Leonardo da Vinci in 1514 and Fausto Veranzio in 1595 worked out such devices on paper. But the first successful chute jump was made in 1797 by the French balloonist, André Garnerin. R.J.J.

Paraffin (PAHR-uh-finn) Paraffin is a colorless, odorless, tasteless wax made from petroleum oil. It is used for sealing jars of jelly and for waxy coating of milk cartons.

SEE: HYDROCARBONS, PETROLEUM

Male (left) and female parakeets

Parakeet Parakeets are brightly colored birds found in warm areas of the Old World and South America. They are small relatives of macaws, cockatoos and PARROTS. Their strong curved beaks are well adapted for cracking seeds. Most nest in holes in trees or termite nests. One species, a gray-breasted parakeet, builds apartment houses of sticks.

Parakeets are more numerous in Australia than anywhere else. They are sometimes pests because they feed in flocks in grain fields or fruit trees. There are very beautiful species in Africa, India and Ceylon, such as the *blossom-headed parakeet* with its pink and violet head and blue and yellow tail. In Australia and New Zealand are large broadtailed species which live on the ground.

The only North American species, the *Carolina parakeet,* has been extinct since 1920. These green and yellow birds were numerous along river bottoms until civilization changed their environment.

Parakeets are easily bred in captivity. The *budgerigar* ("budgie") or *shell parakeet* of Australia is a popular pet. In its wild state it feeds in flocks near the waterholes of the dry Australian grasslands. When domesticated it can be taught to imitate speech, whistle and eat from a hand.   E.R.B.

Parallax Parallax is what seems to be a change in position of a distant object caused by a shift in the position of the observer. In observations of stars, parallax is the result of the earth's rotation moving the observer.
SEE: MATHEMATICS, STAR

Parallel Parallel refers to lines or planes which extend in the same direction and at the same distance apart at all points. Parallel lines or planes never meet, no matter how far extended. Some LEAVES have parallel veins.

Paralysis (puh-RAL-uh-sis) Paralysis is a condition of the body in which muscles fail to function. It may be caused by a birth defect, a disease, a tumor growth, or poisoning.

Muscles contract when they are stimulated by an impulse. Impulses are carried by nerve fibers originating in the BRAIN or SPINAL CORD. Any destruction of the *motor cells* of the brain will cause paralysis. Such destruction can be caused by a brain hemorrhage or a tumor.

A nerve fiber is like a wire connecting a motor cell from the spinal cord or brain to a muscle. If a nerve is cut, there will be paralysis of the muscle connected to it. Infections of the covering of the spinal cord (MENINGITIS) or its motor cells (POLIO) will cause paralysis. Degeneration of the nerve insulation (myelin) causes a different kind of paralysis, as in MULTIPLE SCLEROSIS. Fatal paralysis of the breathing muscles can be caused by chemicals such as *parathion,* an insecticide.   B.M.H./E.S.S.
SEE ALSO: MUSCULAR DYSTROPHY, POLIOMYELITIS

Paramecium (pair-uh-MEE-see-um) The paramecium is a slipper-shaped, one-celled animal. This microscopic animal has tiny hair-like structures, called *cilia,* all over its surface. The best known kind, *Paramecium caudatum,* is widely used in schools for the study of PROTOZOA.

The fresh-water paramecia can be collected in the underwater weeds of ponds. These weeds, covered with pond-water in a glass jar, will decay after standing at room

One-celled paramecia, such as may be found in many ponds
Photo-micrographs by
National Teaching Aids, Inc.

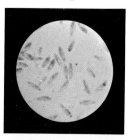

✳ THINGS TO DO

HOW DO PARAMECIA REACT TO THEIR SURROUNDINGS?

1 Paramecia may be obtained from a supply house or from a homemade culture (see PROTOZOA). Place a few drops of the solution they come in on a glass slide. Put a few minute crystals of carmine in the edge of the drop of water.

2 Place the slide on a microscope and bring the paramecia into focus. A powerful hand lens will work almost as well if a microscope is not available. Observe the paramecia as they approach the crystals. The movement of the cilia causes them to roll, go forward and to back up.

3 Continue to experiment with different materials, starting each time with a fresh culture on the slide. Place a small chip of ice in one place in the drop of water. Which way will the paramecia turn? Cover one-half of the slide to eliminate the light. Do they prefer darkness? Connect a wire to each terminal of a dry cell. Touch the exposed ends of the wires together in part of the solution. A very slight current will be discharged. Can these little one-celled animals respond to an electrical charge? Paramecia, though lacking a nervous system, are still very responsive to their environment.

temperature for two to three days. The scum which forms on the surface will contain dozens of paramecia.

The paramecium's shape never changes. Its front end is blunt and its posterior pointed. About one-third of the way from the front is an oral groove lined with cilia. This groove ends in a *cell pharynx.* Bacteria, the paramecium's food, are swept into the mouth by the cilia in the groove and are enclosed in a bubble-like structure called a *food vacuole.* Digestion occurs in the vacuole as it moves in a set pattern through the cell. Undigested material is discharged from a point at the end of the cell called the *anal pore.*

The paramecium has two nuclei, the larger called the *macronucleus,* the smaller, the *micronucleus.* The micronucleus controls reproduction, the macronucleus, all other functions. *Trichocysts,* small glassy rod-shaped bodies just below the surface, are used for defense and for anchoring the animal. The cilia move food in and move the animal forward. Cilia are connected by threads inside the body, and beat in unison like many small oars. The paramecium avoids objects in its path by trial and error. When it strikes an obstacle, it backs up, changes direction and tries again. A contractile vacuole forms every ten to twenty minutes to expel excess water from the cell.

The paramecium divides crosswise, by mitosis, after the nuclei divide and a second cell pharynx buds off. *Conjugation,* a simple form of sexual reproduction, can also take place. Two paramecia lie with their oral grooves touching. The macronuclei of each disintegrate; the micronuclei of each divide twice, forming four micronuclei. Three disintegrate and one divides into stationary and migratory nuclei. The migratory nuclei are exchanged and unite with the stationary nucleus of the other cell.

The individuals separate and each divides to form four new individuals.   J. K. L.

SEE ALSO: MITOSIS and MEIOSIS; REPRODUCTION, ASEXUAL

Parasites A host is a person who allows guests to share his home and food. Although most guests are pleasant, some can be very selfish. Those which take all that they can from their host are called *parasites.* Many plants and animals are parasites which feed upon other living plants and animals. They accept food and a home from their host. In return they offer only sickness and disease.

Houses for people are large enough to permit many kinds of plants and animals to live together. In one house there may be ants, geraniums, dogs, molds, moths, and people. To most parasites the body of the host is as large as a building. Parasites are always smaller than their host. Many cannot be seen except under a microscope. Thus, many thousands of parasites may live in one host.

Parasites often choose to live inside other parasites. A virus may live in a bacterium, which lives in a worm, which lives in a dog. One dog may be host to many kinds of parasites.

The word *parasite* really means "alongside food." Parasitism is concerned mainly with the problem of obtaining food. Certain plants and animals have found it easier to become parasites than to compete for food. Organisms which feed upon other plants and animals do not always find quantities of food. Parasitism flourishes among viruses, non-green plants, and animal groups.

PARASITIC PLANTS AND ANIMALS

A true parasite feeds only upon living plants and animals. Plants which feed upon dead or decaying matter are called *saprophytes,* while animals which feed upon dead organisms are called *scavengers.* A few parasites, like the blue-green mold on the orange, are able to live upon either dead or living hosts. Green plants, which contain chlorophyll, like the mistletoe, are able to manufacture part of their own food. Since they cannot manufacture enough food, they become *semi-parasites* upon larger plants.

There are parasitic members of nearly all

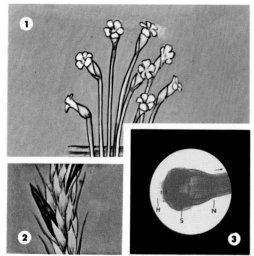

Courtesy Society For Visual Education, Inc.
1—Cancerroot, a parasitic plant, lives on the roots of other plants
2—Ergot on rye is also caused by bacteria
Photo-micrograph by National Teaching Aids, Inc.
3—Head of a tapeworm shows the hooked mouth of this parasite.

phyla of both plants and animals. Many plant parasites are found among the *bacteria, slime molds,* and *true fungi.* Diseases of man, such as tuberculosis and pneumonia, as well as rots and galls of plants are caused by bacteria. Several molds cause infection of animals. Aquarium goldfish are often killed with water mold, while man may develop skin diseases caused by black mold. The fungi cause damage to higher plants by producing rusts, mildews, smuts, and rots. Such diseases as potato blight, Dutch elm disease, and apple scab result from attachment by these parasites. In man, ringworm and athlete's foot, caused by the same organism, are fungus diseases.

Animal parasites attack almost every species of animal. Parasitic species number in the tens of thousands. The greatest number of parasitic animals are found among the *protozoan, flatworm, roundworm* and *arthropod* phyla. In man, yellow fever, sleeping sickness, and amebic dysentery are caused by members of the *Protozoa.* The fluke, tapeworm, trichina, and filaria are a few of the parasitic worms that cause disease to many higher animals. By sucking cell sap, some roundworms cause wilting and gall in plants. Lice, mites, and ticks are well-known parasites among the arthropods. With greater powers of locomotion, higher animals are better equipped to compete for food. Only a few, such as the LAMPREY eel, adopt parasitic habits.

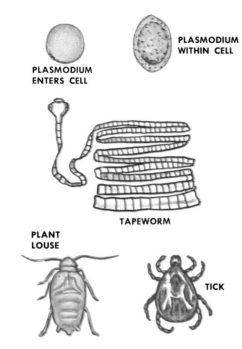

PLASMODIUM
ENTERS CELL

PLASMODIUM
WITHIN CELL

TAPEWORM

PLANT
LOUSE

TICK

Some common parasites

Buchsbaum

The leech has suckers which cling to skin

METHODS OF ATTACK AND DEFENSE

A soldier in the army must have special equipment to invade the enemy camp. In the same way, all parasites must have special body parts to enable them to live as unwelcome guests within the host. Each species has its own equipment for attack.

Those which attach themselves to the outer surface are called *outer* or *ectoparasites*. Animals like the leeches, mites, and lamprey eels, which cling to skin or hair, have developed suckers and hooks. Many have cutting, biting, or sucking mouth parts. Plants like the molds, fungi, dodder, and mistletoe have rootlike structures called *haustoria* which pierce the outer tissue of the host and draw nourishment from the inner cells.

Plants and animals which live inside the body of the host are called *inner* or *endoparasites*. They must have defenses against digestive juices, antibodies, white blood cells, and acids. Those like the viruses, bacteria, and fungi which move into the cells and feed directly upon the cell protoplasm develop thick outer coverings. Parasitic worms have thick cuticles, while many have additional hooks and suckers. Endoparasites often produce enzymes which break down the tissue and provide a pathway for movement.

Since the body changes in function, many parasites are no longer able to live independently. Many adults lose important body parts. The tapeworm, for example, loses its digestive, muscular, and nervous systems. One parasitic barnacle loses its shell so that it no longer resembles a barnacle.

Since parasites do not have to worry about locomotion, digestion, or protection, they are able to concentrate all their efforts upon reproduction. Most of them have well-developed reproductive systems and are able to produce quantities of young. One fluke, for example, may produce thousands of eggs. However, parasites must be prolific since many of the young never reach the proper host.

MOVEMENT FROM HOST TO HOST

Many animal parasites are able to move freely, either in the larva or the adult stage. For example, the larva of the hookworm is free to move to find a host, while the adult is completely parasitic. But organisms like the bacteria, viruses, and molds must rely upon wind, water, or an intermediate host like the mosquito to transfer them from host to host. These organisms lack the power of locomotion.

Many parasites need to have two or more hosts in order to complete their life cycles. Since they alternate in order from one host to the next, this method is called *alternation of host*. They rely upon both food chains and physical agents like wind, air, and water.

The wheat rust has two hosts. Carried by the wind, the spores are passed to the barberry, where they undergo development. The Chinese liver fluke has two intermediate hosts. The adult, which lives in the liver of man, sheds eggs into the intestine. These are passed with the feces to the ground. After being eaten by a snail, they are able to develop into larvae which swim through the water, find a fish, and settle in the muscle tissue. Man is the third host, if he eats raw or undercooked fish. E. P. L.

SEE ALSO: BACTERIA, BALANCE OF NATURE, BLIGHT, FILARIA, FUNGUS, HOOKWORM, LIVER FLUKE, MOLDS, PINWORM, PROTOZOA, TAPEWORM, TRICHINA, VIRUS

Parasympathetic see Autonomic nervous system, Nervous system

Parathyroid (par-uh-THY-royd) The parathyroid is a special gland in the body. There are actually four parathyroid glands. Two pairs of these tiny pea-shaped structures rest on the back of the THYROID gland. The parathyroid glands secrete a hormone called *parathormone*.

Parathormone controls the amount of calcium and phosphorus in the blood and the way in which these minerals are used by the body. Normally there is a balance in the body between the level of calcium and phosphorus. When there is too little parathyroid hormone, there is a rise in the level of phosphorus in the blood and a drop in the level of calcium. If blood calcium is markedly decreased, a condition called *tetany* occurs. In such cases, the muscles of the body become irritable and contract, producing spasms throughout the body. The muscles of the larynx may be involved and obstruct the passage of air from outside into the lungs. The muscles controlling breathing go into spasm. Death results in severe cases. Accidental removal of the parathyroid glands during surgery can produce the same effect.

Oversecretion of the parathyroids is called *hyperparathyroidism*. It may be caused by tumors of the glands or by other disturbances of calcium-phosphorus metabolism. The blood level of calcium rises and the level of phosphorus falls. In such a condition there is a loss of calcium from the bones. This calcium loss causes a weakening of the bone structure. Bone pain, fractures, bone deformities, kidney stones, and nephritis often result. G. A. D.

SEE ALSO: ENDOCRINE GLANDS

Paré, Ambroise (pah-RAY, ahm-BRWAHZ) (1510-1590) Paré was a French barber-surgeon who became the greatest surgeon of the Renaissance. He later became known as the "father of modern surgery."

During Paré's lifetime France was at war against Italy, Germany, and England, and later against the French Huguenots at home. After three years at the Paris Hospital, he joined the French army and saw military service for the next thirty years. He performed so many operations of every sort on so many men that he developed new techniques and methods of treating wounds. He invented artery forceps and other types of surgical instruments.

In 1554 Ambroise Paré was made a member of the College of St. Come, the most important surgical society of France at the time. D.H.J.

Paregoric (par-uh-GORE-ick) Paregoric is the name for a preparation containing a small amount of OPIUM, ANISE oil, benzoic acid, honey, dilute alcohol, and camphor. It is used in the treatment of DIARRHEA and as a pain reliever.

SEE: NARCOTICS

Parícutin Volcano Parícutin is a famous VOLCANO that erupted in Mexico in 1943. It began as a hot spot in a cornfield and eventually built up a cinder cone 1,378 feet (420 meters) high.

Parícutin is a volcano of the type called a cinder cone. It has a typical cone-shape appearance, the result of an accumulation of ash and cinder. Parícutin was active 9 years, during which it grew from a 30-foot (9-meter) to a 1,378-foot (420-meter) cone. Its crater had an 856-foot (270-meter) diameter. Lava poured out from the base of the cone several times, producing a lava field of .9 square mile (2.3 square kilometers). Scientists were able to observe all periods of its eruptive phase from birth to death. P.P.S.

Paris green see Arsenic

WHITE-CRESTED COCKATOO

SULFUR-CRESTED COCKATOO

LEADBEATER'S COCKATOO

MACAW

TRUE PARROT

CAROLINA PARAKEET

Parkinson's disease This is a disease of a part of the brain, possibly due to an early childhood virus infection. It causes muscle stiffness and weakness with shaking (tremor). It is sometimes called *shaking palsy*.

The disease rarely affects people less than fifty or sixty years old. There is a rigidity of the muscles and a rhythmical "pill rolling" tremor of the fingers and hands. The face loses emotion expression and appears fixed. The eyes blink infrequently and appear to stare. The affected person walks in a stooped position and takes short, quick steps. He appears to be falling forward, often going faster and faster to prevent a loss of balance. Muscle response to commands from the brain may be slowed.

The disease is chronic. As it progresses, the person may need help when getting out of a chair. Dressing, shaving, and writing become difficult. The tremor disappears during sleep, but it is present when the person is awake and his muscles are relaxed. The tremor will slow down or disappear when the hand is used. This distinguishes Parkinson's disease from diseases or tumors of the cerebellum, in which a tremor appears *when* the hand is used. These symptoms are due to degeneration of the nerve cells at the base of the brain. Only the motor system is affected. Sensations of heat, cold, or pain are normal. The intellect, or thinking process, also remains normal.

B.M.H.

Parrot Parrots and their relatives, the macaws, parakeets and lories, make up a large family. They are brightly colored birds ranging from warbler to eagle size, with strong, hooked beaks and hawk-like heads. The upper jaw moves up so that the beak can work like pliers, crushing the parrot's food.

Parrots can be divided into two groups depending on whether their thick, fleshy tongues are fringed or blunt. The former eat nectars and fruit juices and the latter eat seeds and nuts. One branch of parrots, the lorikeets, crush blossoms and lick up the sticky nectar with their tongues.

Parrots use their feet as hands to eat. Two of the four toes are turned backward. They are either left- or right-handed. They are good climbers, using their beaks to help.

Most species nest in holes in trees but a few build stick nests. The male helps the female incubate the eggs for three weeks and the young hatch out blind and naked. Most species feed their young on partly digested food.

Men have made pets of parrots since ancient times. They are the best talkers in the animal kingdom and are good at voice mimicry. As pets, they may live from 50 to 80 years. At one time when it was found they carried *psittacosis,* or parrot fever, their popularity declined but now an antibiotic is available which will cure birds of this disease. E. R. B.

SEE ALSO: ANIMAL DISEASES, MACAW, PARAKEET

Parrot fever see Animal diseases, Parrot

Parsec A parsec, a unit of length, is used by astronomers. A parsec is a

1250

very large unit, equal to 3.08 x 10^{12} kilometers, or 1.91 trillion miles.

Parsley
This HERB usually lives for a period of two years and then dies. It grows to be about 2 feet (.6 meter) tall. Leafy and sweet, it is used in modern cooking for flavoring and decoration.

Dark green, lacy LEAVES are finely divided or lobed. The small, greenish FLOWERS are perfect, forming umbrella-shaped clusters on a single stalk. Five sepals form a tube around the 5 petals and 5 stamens. A single pistil is composed of 2 chambers or carpels. The ovary develops into a dry FRUIT which is classified as a schizocarp.

Parsley is a good source of vitamins A and C. It belongs to the family Umbelliferae, commonly called the parsley family.   H.J.C.

Parsnip
Parsnip is a flowering HERB with a coarse, hollow stem. Its taproot is dull white and sweet, shaped like a carrot, and eaten as a VEGETABLE.

Parsnip grows best in cool, temperate climates, and its flavor improves when it is left in the winter soil or stored in a cold place for a while. Parsnip seeds can be planted in the spring. Although they germinate slowly, by fall they may grow to be over 1 foot (.3 meter) tall.

Parsnip belongs to the family Umbelliferae which is commonly called the celery, carrot, or parsnip family.   H.J.C.

Parthenocarpy
(pahr-thuh-noh-CARP-ee) Parthenocarpy is the development of FRUIT without seeds. Bananas, navel oranges, pineapples, and green grapes do this naturally.

Man can produce fruit without seeds by using certain synthetic growth chemicals. The ovary is stimulated to mature, but no ovules develop. Use of these synthetic chemicals is producing seedless cucumbers, melons, and tomatoes.   H. J. C.

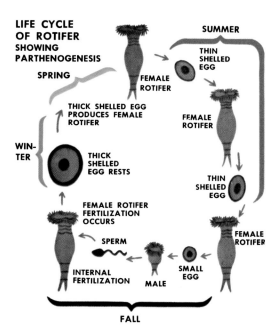

A rotifer's life cycle illustrates parthenogenesis

Parthenogenesis
(pahr-thuh-noh-JENN-uh-siss) Parthenogenesis is a type of reproduction in which a new organism develops from an egg which has not united with a sperm. In animals, it occurs naturally in *rotifers*, a type of worm, in BEES and APHIDS, and in water fleas. Some algae and fungi also reproduce parthenogenetically. Eggs of many invertebrates and of frogs have been developed without fertilization through artificial stimulation of the eggs by pricking, shaking, and changing the kind of solution they are in. Occasionally parthenogenesis occurs naturally in all major groups of animals except the vertebrates and echinoderms and in all plants except mosses and liverworts.

Parthenogenesis is the sole means of reproduction only in a few aphids and parasitic insects. In other groups males are produced periodically, usually in the fall. They fertilize eggs which are capable of surviving the winter. These eggs in turn produce females which reproduce parthenogenetic females until the next fall.

A slightly different parthenogenetic reproduction occurs in bees. The queen bee is the sole egg-producing female. It mates once with a drone and stores the sperm in its body. The fertilized eggs which it produced develop into queen bees or workers (infertile females). It also lays unfertilized eggs which have half the number of chromosomes of the female bees. These develop parthenogenetically into the male drones.   J. K. L.
SEE ALSO: REPRODUCTION, ASEXUAL; REPRODUCTIVE SYSTEMS; ROTIFERA

Particle see Nuclear particles

Particle detector Charged atomic or NUCLEAR PARTICLES are detected when passed through a particle detector. The charged particles create an electrical disturbance which can be observed, as in the Wilson CLOUD CHAMBER, or recorded, as in the Geiger-Müller counter.
SEE: GEIGER COUNTER

Particulate matter Particulate matter is made of small solid particles and fine liquid droplets in the air. There is a wide range in their size. Particulate matter can damage the lungs.

Particulate matter has many sources. Spray from ocean waves produces salt particles. Volcanic eruptions produce mineral particles. Spores, viruses, pollen, and bacteria are biological airborne particles. Man is a major producer of particulate matter. The use of carbon fuels and industrial processes release millions of tons of particles each year.

The sizes of airborne particles vary greatly. Viruses are .006 to .02 micrometers (μ m). Metallurgical dust ranges from .001 μ m to 100 μ m. Fog ranges from 1 μ m to 50 μ m. Fire ash ranges from 1 μ m to 1,000 μ m.

Particulate matter causes physiological damage to the lungs. The larger particles are captured in the nose, but smaller particles can go into the lungs, where they can damage cells or be absorbed by the body.
A.J.H.

SEE ALSO: AIR POLLUTION

Partridge see Fowl, Grouse, Quail

Parturition Parturition is the act of giving BIRTH to young. It begins with contractions of the uterus which force the infant out of the uterus and through the vagina, and it ends with the delivery of the placenta.
SEE: REPRODUCTION, SEXUAL

Pasqueflower see Wild flowers

Passion flower see Plants, tropical

Pasteur, Louis (1822-1895) Louis Pasteur was the French chemist who became known as the "father of bacteriology." He was the first scientist to discover how to prevent the spread of diseases caused by INFECTION. He proved that the microscopic organisms found in liquids after a chemical change (a process known as FERMENTATION) come from the air. He also discovered that they could be killed, thus preventing the spread of disease. The process he discovered to kill these germs in milk and dry wines by heating the liquid to a point just below the boiling point and then cooling it rapidly is called *pasteurization*.

In 1849, Pasteur was invited to serve on the Faculty of Sciences as the professor of chemistry at Strasbourg, and it was there that he began his research on fermentation. There he first showed that certain organic chemicals made by plants exist in two light-polarizing varieties. The improvements he eventually brought about in winemaking are said to have saved France enough money to pay its indemnity to Prussia at the close of the Franco-Prussian War.

In 1854, Pasteur became the Dean of the new Faculty of the Sciences at Lille. Although his administrative duties, combined with his teaching responsibilities, made a heavy load, he consented to make a thorough study of a disease threatening to destroy the silkworms in France. For five years he carried on intensive research, and eventually discovered the parasite causing the trouble. This gift to France saved the entire silk industry of the country.

Milk is put into sterilized bottles (left) after being pasteurized by this machine

Pasteur's second great claim to fame (after pasteurization) is his work in medicine, especially his development of a vaccine against rabies. While experimenting with chicken cholera, he stumbled upon the principle of using killed or weakened viruses to make animals resistant to diseases. This principle is called *immunization.* He next applied the idea to anthrax, a disease that attacks cattle and sheep. Then he began looking for the germ that causes rabies. The disease, sometimes called *hydrophobia,* was known to be transmitted by the bites of animals that were sick with it. A dog that had rabies was called a "mad dog," and was terribly feared because the disease was usually fatal. Pasteur developed a vaccine against it, and his first human patient, nine-year-old Joseph Meister, recovered.

Even more dramatically, 16 out of 19 Russian peasants who had been bitten by a mad wolf were saved by Pasteur's injections, despite the fact that the treatment was not started until 19 days after they were bitten. They had had to come all the way from Russia. In recognition, the Czar donated 100,000 francs toward the building of the Pasteur Institute. This institution, built by contributions of people in every land, is a living monument to Pasteur. He served as its director from 1888 until he died in 1895.   D. A. B.

SEE ALSO: MEDICINE, PASTEURIZATION

Pasteurization (pass-ter-ih-ZAY-shun) After milk leaves the farm and goes to the dairy, it goes through a process called pasteurization. This process destroys dangerous disease-causing microorganisms.

Pasteurized milk has been heated and held at a given temperature for a certain length of time. This can be accomplished in two ways. The milk may be heated to about 143° F. (61.7° C.) and held at that temperature for 30 minutes, or it may be heated to 160° F. (71.1° C.) and held there for about 16 seconds. The process destroys most microorganisms and spares the flavor of the milk, which higher temperatures would affect. The same process is also applied to wines.

Microorganisms, too small to be seen without a microscope, are the cause of tuberculosis, typhoid fever, dysentery, undulant fever, diphtheria, scarlet fever, and septic sore throat. Pasteurization prevents the spread of disease through the milk supply.

Pasteurization does not kill all the microorganisms present in milk. Many bacteria still live, but these are not harmful to the body. Milk is tested from samples taken from each source. The city or county health department is responsible for this task, and milk is graded according to the bacteria count and number of coloform organisms in each milliliter.

Unpasteurized milk may still be sold in some communities, but it must be used more quickly than milk which is pasteurized. Almost all milk sold in stores is Grade A pasteurized. Lower grades of milk are used in making powdered milk or cheeses as the bacteria will be destroyed by cooking or chemical treatment.   V. V. N.

SEE ALSO: BACTERIOLOGY; DAIRY PRODUCTS; PASTEUR, LOUIS

Patella see Skeleton

A pathologist tests body fluids and tissues to help doctors make a diagnosis of a disease.

Pathology (puh-THAHL-uh-jee) Pathology is the branch of medical science which considers the changes of function and the changes of structure brought about by disease.

General pathology is that division of pathology which studies those abnormal processes caused in different organs of the body by diseases. An example of such a change is that found in an inflammation showing redness, swelling, heat, and pain.

Humoral pathology, an older science introduced by HIPPOCRATES (460 B.C.-355 B.C.) attributed the cause of disease to an abnormal condition of the blood. *Cellular* pathology, which was formulated about 1840, considered the cell as the basis for all living phenomena. Today pathology recognizes both the humoral and cellular concepts.

Other subdivisions of pathology are *pathologic physiology,* which deals with disturbances of function in disease; *morphologic* pathology which deals with the study of structural changes in disease; and *special* pathology, covering special diseases.

The study of pathologic physiology received its first great impetus about 1830 to 1840 from Karl Rokitansky, professor of Pathological Anatomy in Vienna. Rokitansky had tremendous experience, having performed 30,000 autopsies during his lifetime. He emphasized, however, that medicine wished to understand the living, rather than dead, organs. Because of his background he was a genius in presenting a pathologic description of diseased parts, in promoting an understanding of the *pathogenesis* (development) of disease, and, then, in correlating anatomy with the symptoms of the disease.

Rudolph Ludwig Virchow (1821-1902) was the father of cellular pathology. Because the humoral theory had held sway for almost 2000 years, introduction of cellular pathology was courageous as well as progressive. Virchow's thesis stated that the seat of disease should be sought in the cell. This concept not only replaced the older humoral theory, but it did not restrict study to gross material, and required a more thorough investigation of microscopic, cellular changes. Virchow taught in Berlin until 1849, but his political utterances demanding improved health conditions antagonized Bismarck, who was the outstanding Prussian politician of his day; and he was forced to leave.

By correlating studies of tissue and organs removed during surgical operations and studies of disease in the living body, the pathologists learn something of the life processes.

Fever, for instance, is a pathologic change caused, in most cases, by the presence of poisonous substances called *toxins* in the blood acting upon the heat centers within the brain. These substances may be bacterial poisons, metabolic products, end products of protein digestion, or ferments. Toxins are also produced by injury, by direct exposure to heat as in sunstroke, by starvation, or even by hysteria. Any infectious process within the body may produce fever.

Presently, medical doctors who are *pathologists* have two major areas of responsibility. One is the running of laboratories *(clinical pathology),* where blood and urine specimens are taken from patients and examined for normal or abnormal substances. (For example, too much sugar in the blood, or any in the urine, is a sign of diabetes mellitus.) The other area is *cellular pathology*—examining tissues from living patients for such things as cancer and tuberculosis, and examining tissue from dead people *(necropsy)* to determine the cause of death. To do this, the pathologist must be able to examine specimens and organs with the naked eye (gross analysis) and with a microscope, after cutting and staining very thin sections of tissue (microscopic analysis.)

The trained pathologist must be not only a practical clinician, he must also have a basic knowledge of human and comparative anatomies, of histology, physiology, embryology, biochemistry, and bacteriology. The knowledge of his field thus serves the future of clinical medicine.   H.K.S./E.S.S.

SEE ALSO: MEDICINE, PHYSIOLOGY

Pauling, Linus (1901-) Pauling, a famous U.S. chemist, won the 1954 NOBEL PRIZE in chemistry. He studied the molecular structure of PROTEIN. He received the 1962 Nobel Peace Prize for opposing nuclear weapons testing.

Linus Pauling became renowned as a brilliant chemist early in his career. Active in research and teaching, he applied the techniques of quantum mechanics and X ray diffraction to determining molecular structures. He did extensive research on the chemical bond. He developed the theory of *resonance* in chemical bonds. He has researched molecular structures of amino acids and proteins. His studies have spanned the fields of physics, chemistry, biology, and medicine. Pauling has conducted important research relative to hereditary diseases. His work led to the discovery of abnormal hemoglobin in persons with SICKLE-CELL ANEMIA.   A.J.H.

Pavlov, Ivan Petrovich (1849-1936) Ivan Pavlov was a Russian doctor (physiologist) who is now remembered for his work on conditioned reflexes in dogs. He discovered that if he always rang a bell each time he fed a dog, the dog would continue to react to the bell even when food was withheld. He was awarded the NOBEL PRIZE for his work on digestion.

Pavlov's work was in three basic areas: circulation of the blood, action of the digestive glands, and formation of conditioned reflexes. His research on techniques causing neuroses in dogs laid the foundation for scientific study of mental illness in humans.

Pavlov achieved world-wide fame as his writings were translated into German, French, and English.   D.H.J.

SEE ALSO: PSYCHOLOGY

Pawpaw see Papaya

Garden pea plant and pod

Pea The garden pea is an annual, climbing herb. The green or yellow seeds formed in pods are used as a vegetable. *Pea* also refers to a large family of plants (*Leguminosae*) which includes locust trees, mesquite shrubs and peanut plants.

Garden peas have hollow stems, white flowers which are self pollinated and fruit classified as LEGUMES. The roots develop nodules containing nitrogen-fixing bacteria. Field peas are hardy plants used mainly for stockfeed. The pigeon or cajan pea is gaining popularity as food for poultry, humans and livestock.

The pea is the plant that MENDEL experimented with in doing his well-known work in breeding and genetics.   H. J. C.

Peach The peach tree bears fruit that has one large seed. The tree grows until it is about 25 feet (7.6 meters) tall. The leaves are long and narrow. The flower is pinkish.

The peach tree, a member of the rose family, is native to China and has been cultivated for over 4000 years. It produces

Peaches, ready for picking
U.S. Department of Agriculture photo

best in regions where the winters are mild and the temperature rarely goes below -10° F. (-23.3° C.). Many peach trees grow in the wild state.

Botanically, the fruit is classified as a DRUPE. The outer fruit wall is fleshy with a stony endocarp surrounding the seed. The pit is grooved. Peaches are of the *free stone* or the *cling* variety. The *Elberta peach* is most widely grown. The tree starts to bear fruit after 3 or 4 years of growth. The flower and fruit appear on the new branches each year. A volatile and fixed oil is extracted from the seed. Brandy is made from the fruit.

Leaf curl, brown rot, scab, peach borer and oriental fruit moth are the most serious pests of this plant.

Nectarines are a variety of peach. The fruit is smaller, more solid and the exocarp is smooth.   H.J.C.

SEE ALSO: FRUIT

Peacock Peacock is the name for the male peafowl. The peafowl is related to other fowl, such as quails, pheasants, and chickens. Almost all zoos have peacocks, many wandering free, because they are easily domesticated and very beautiful.

The peacock of India and Malaya is a large green and blue bird with long naked legs and a small crested head. A distant cousin discovered recently in the Congo is glossy black with a white tuft in its crown.

Wild peacocks live in groups in open forests, roosting at night in trees. The male courtship display consists of raising the upper long tail

Peacock, the male peafowl

coverts into a fan which reaches the ground on both sides. The feather surfaces are covered with many thin layers of horn which reflect and refract light, making the colors iridescent. Yellowish spots add to the beauty. These tail coverts develop in the male's third year. Each male has a harem of two to five smaller and duller females. The buff-colored eggs are laid in a crude nest on the ground.   E. R. B.

SEE ALSO: FOWL

Peafowl see Peacock

Peanuts see Legume, Nuts

Pear leaves, fruit and flower

Pear The pear tree has been grown for over 4000 years. It is a member of the rose family. In the United States, most pears are grown in the northwestern states. These trees cannot stand extremes of temperature change as apple trees can, therefore they are rather limited to certain regions.

The leaves of the pear tree have serrated margins. The flower has five petals and five carpels and is generally white. The flower is perfect, meaning that both male and female parts are present. The fruit is classified as *accessory* since much of the wall is the fleshy receptacle. The grittiness of the fruit is caused by the presence of minute stone cells or *schlerenchyma* tissue.

Propagation is done by seeds or grafting. The dwarf pear is grafted onto a slow growing rootstock such as quince. Besides using the fruit as food, man extracts oil from the seeds. A drink called *perry* is made from the fruit juice.   H. J. C.

Pearl A pearl is a gem made by certain animals that live within shells. These animals are *mollusks*. A pearl is formed when a grain of sand or other small object gets between the hard outer shell and the inner coat, called the *mantle*.

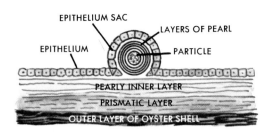

Formation of a pearl

Admiral Robert E. Peary

The mollusk surrounds the irritation with *nacre,* a secretion from the mantle. This is the same substance that lines the oyster's shell and is called *mother-of-pearl.* Many thin layers of nacre give a pearl its luster. The result is a sore spot for the oyster but a beautiful jewel for man.

The biggest pearl oysters are found in the South Seas. The Persian Gulf yields a yellowish pearl. Some may be pink, bluish, gray, or black. The coasts of Australia, Venezuela, Malaya, Mexico, and lower California are other important sources of pearls. Many mollusks produce pearls, but only two types produce precious pearls. These are the genera *Meleagrina* of the tropical seas and *Unio* of fresh water streams.

The average pearl takes about 7 years for its development. Its value is determined by its size and luster. The largest pearl ever found was about 2 inches (5 centimeters) in diameter. *Cultured* pearls are real pearls but the original nucleus was inserted by man. They are not as costly as true pearls.

Unfortunately, pearls are perishable. Sunlight and skin acids are injurious to them. Pearls should be kept clean and wrapped in moist coverings when not in use. With care, they last over a hundred years.   J.A.D.

SEE ALSO: GEM, MOLLUSCA

Peary, Robert Edwin (1856-1920)

Robert Peary was the American explorer who discovered the North Pole. From soundings taken, he also discovered that the sea around the North Pole was not as shallow as was popularly believed up until that time.

Peary was born in Pennsylvania, but his family soon returned to Maine, where his ancestors had lived. He attended Bowdoin College where he took the civil engineering course. He worked first as a land surveyor in Maine and then as a draftsman for the U.S. Coast and Geodetic Survey. He passed the difficult examination for civil engineers in the U.S. Navy and took up his lifelong career in engineering, from which he took leaves of absence when he went on his Arctic explorations. He first worked on ship canals and dry docks. When a canal was being planned across Central America, Peary was sent to survey the possibility of a route across Nicaragua. He is often credited with being one of the first engineers to recommend that the canal be dug through the Isthmus of Panama, as it later was.

His first four Arctic journeys were in Greenland. His wife went with him on several of these expeditions, and their first child, Marie, was born in Greenland, further north than any but Eskimo children had ever been born before. Peary was not the first man to cross Greenland, as another explorer, Nansen, beat him by a small margin, but he made many useful discoveries. He established the fact that Greenland is an island; he found and brought back three enormous meteorites; and he made friends with the Eskimos and learned to use their methods and clothing.

With the knowledge gained from the Greenland explorations, Peary set his sights on reaching the North Pole. His plan was to sail a ship as far north as it could go along the Greenland coast, and push on with dogs and sledges. Twelve years, three expeditions, two ships and seven frostbitten toes later, he achieved his goal. At his side when he planted five flags at the North Pole were his assistant Matthew Henson, who accompanied him on nearly all these trips, and four Eskimos. And behind their achievement stood Robert Bartlett, captain of the ship *Roosevelt,* and all the men who had been working in relays to break trail, build igloos, and bring up supplies so that Peary and his adventurous companions could not only get to the North Pole, but also come back to civilization alive.

Another explorer, Frederick A. Cook, claimed to have reached the Pole first, but after a Congressional investigation, it was decided that Cook had probably not reached it at all.   D.A.B.

Sphagnum moss is the common moss of peat bogs

J. W. Thompson

Peccary, or javelina

Peat During the early stages of the earth's development, plants such as mosses and ferns grew thickly in many swamps and BOGS. As the plants died, their remains sank to the bottom and new plants grew on top of them. Great masses of half-decayed brown, spongy material formed. This is peat. If there had been more pressure and heat from the great amounts of sand and clay that were gradually piled on the peat, the peat would have changed into coal.

The wet marshy ground where peat is found is called a *peat bog*. The water in a peat bog is acid and preserves plants that fall into it. Botanists are able to identify plants that grew in peat bogs centuries ago. The most common type found is the large sphagnum.

Most of the peat deposits were formed during the Carboniferous Age. Mosses, giant ferns and ancient conifer-like plants became bogged down in stagnant swamps. When these were covered with clay, they were more or less hardened into peat, lignite or harder COAL.

Peat has many uses. It is used as a FUEL even though it leaves ten times more ash than most other fuels. It holds water well and so is used for surgical dressings, soil conditioners and a propagating medium.   H. J. C.
SEE ALSO: MOSS

Pecan see Hickory, Nuts

Peccary (PEK-ar-e) The peccary is a hoofed, tailless, piglike animal with tusks that turn downward. It is a vicious fighter, and usually travels in herds. The two species, the collared peccary and the white-lipped peccary, are found from Texas to Paraguay.

Pectin (PEK-tin) Pectin is a carbohydrate found in ripe fruits and some vegetables. It dissolves in boiling water and forms a jelly when cooled. Commercial pectin can be bought in stores and used to make jellies. It also has various uses in medicines.

Pedigree A pedigree is a record of a family. It may be of a family of plants, animals, or humans. A person's pedigree is called a *family tree*. It tells the name of parents, grandparents, and ancestors back through the centuries, and gives information of cities and counties where they were known to have lived. Anyone can make a simple family tree.

In animals and plants, pedigrees are of great value in breeding certain desirable characteristics into the offspring. These records of ancestors help to improve varieties of plants and breeds of animals because they tell breeders the kind of offsprings the male and female will have. Two fast horses may produce a winning race horse. A male and female Airedale dog with proper proportions and markings may produce a champion puppy. More perfect and valuable fruits, vegetables, trees, and flowers may be developed when records are kept of the original plants. Pedigrees are a record for controlled breeding, an important science based on Gregor Mendel's laws of heredity.
J. K. K.
SEE ALSO: BREEDING; HYBRIDIZATION; MENDEL, GREGOR

Peewee

A peewee resembles other flycatchers like the yellow-bellied flycatcher.

Peewee The peewee is a member of the flycatcher family, often confused with the phoebe. It is hard to see and can be most easily distinguished by the sad way in which it says its name.

The adult is 6 to 6½ inches (15.2 to 16.5 centimeters) long, dark olive-gray above with a grayish-white breast. The wings are marked with whitish bars. It prefers to live in dry woods, often nesting in orchards. When it is feeding, it perches in the tops of trees and dives for flying insects.

The peewee breeds in eastern North America and winters in South America. The nest is broad and flat and beautifully made. It is covered so that it seems to grow out of a branch.   E.R.B.

SEE ALSO: FLYCATCHER

Pegasus (PEGG-uh-suss) Pegasus is a group of stars that seemed to ancient people to outline the shape of a horse. This CONSTELLATION covers a large area of the sky. It can be found by locating the *Square of Pegasus.* Four bright stars mark the corners of this large square. The square represents the body of the horse. A line of stars ending in a triangle composes his neck and head. The horse is usually upside down. The stars that represent its forefeet usually point upward in the sky. Pegasus does not have any hind legs marked by stars.

Pegasus can be found most easily in autumn and winter. It is near the royal family of constellations—Cassiopeia, Cepheus, Andromeda, and Perseus. In fact, one of the stars of the square is part of the constellation of Andromeda.

Pegasus

According to legend, Pegasus was the winged horse which sprang from the head of Medusa when Perseus killed Medusa. Either Minerva or Neptune tamed Pegasus and gave him to Bellerophon. Pegasus carried his master to Lycia, where Bellerophon slew Chimera, a monster. Jupiter was displeased and sent a gadfly to sting Pegasus. The horse threw Bellerophon and flew up into the sky.   C. L. K.

Pegmatite Pegmatite is a form of coarse-grain igneous ROCK. It usually occurs as *dikes* associated with a large mass of *plutonic* rock of finer grain size. The most common minerals in pegmatites are FELDSPAR, QUARTZ, and MICA. Very often these minerals occur in extremely large sizes and are very valuable to collectors.

Peking man see Evolution of man

Pelagic (puh-LAJ-ick) Pelagic is a term which is used to describe the part of the ocean away from the shore. This is the open sea which lies above the *abyss* or *depths.* The pelagic zone usually refers only to the part of the ocean as far down as sunlight penetrates.

SEE: CURRENTS, OCEAN; GRAND BANKS; MARINE BIOLOGY; OCEAN; PLANKTON; SARGASSUM

The major life zones of the ocean (not drawn to scale)

LITTORAL ZONE

PELAGIC ZONE

ABYSSAL ZONE

F. A. Blashfield

White pelicans

Pelican Pelicans are large, fish-eating birds with large beaks, throat pouches, and webbed feet. Of the ten species of pelicans, two are common in Florida and the Gulf states. One species is white and the other brown. Both brown and white pelicans breed in huge colonies.

Pelicans have a distinctive flight pattern—six or seven wing strokes followed by a short period of soaring. In flocks, the flight pattern is repeated in unison.

The white pelican lives around fresh water in summer and salt water in winter. It catches fish while swimming and never dives. The white pelican's wingspan is 8 or 9 feet (2.4 or 2.7 meters). Its weight is about 16 pounds (7.25 kilograms). Two to four eggs are incubated by both parents. Young are born naked. They feed by removing fish from deep in the mother's pouch.

The brown pelicans always frequent salt water. They catch fish by diving from a height of about 20 feet (6.1 meters). J.C.K.

Pellagra see Vitamin deficiency

Peltier, Jean Charles Athanase (1785-1845) Peltier was a French physicist now remembered as the man who completed a discovery made by T. J. Seebeck. This discovery, made in 1834, revealed that an electric current produces either heating or cooling at the junction place of two different metals. The direction in which the current is traveling determines whether cooling or heating is produced.

In 1961, production of small-sized electric refrigerators using the cooling effect discovered by Peltier was announced. A clockmaker by trade, Peltier was born at Ham,

France, on February 25, 1785. He died in Paris on October 27, 1845. D. H. J.
SEE ALSO: ELECTRICITY, REFRIGERATION

Pelvis The pelvis is the bony ring formed by the two hip bones and the *sacrum* and *coccyx* of the vertebral column. It is also the expanded end of the ureter in the kidney.
SEE ALSO: SKELETON

Pendulum (PEN-juh-luhm) A pendulum can be made by tying a weight, such as a stone, to a string. If the string is held and the weighted end is pushed, the string and weight will swing back and forth. A pendulum is used in certain clocks, in earthquake detectors, and in determining geological mineral deposits.

A simple pendulum has a weight, or *bob*, suspended from a fixed point by a light weight line. The bob swings back and forth in a path called the *arc*. The time it takes for a pendulum bob to swing from one end of the arc to the other and back again is called the *period of the pendulum*. If the length of the line remains the same, the period of the pendulum is affected only by changes in gravity—not by the width of arc.

Certain basic laws apply to a pendulum's period. A pendulum's period is not affected by the weight of the bob unless extreme air resistance exists. A pendulum's period increases as the length of line increases. The pendulum's period is directly proportional to the square root of the length of the pendulum's line. It is inversely proportional to the square root of the ACCELERATION due to gravity (g). In other words, short pendulums have short periods and swing rapidly. Pendulums with long lines have long periods

The changing length of the pendulum's string produces the different periods on the pendulum's swing

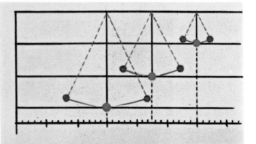

and swing slowly. In a pendulum clock, if the clock runs too rapidly, one lengthens or lowers the pendulum bob. If the clock runs too slowly, one shortens or raises the pendulum bob.

The *Foucault* pendulum, developed in 1851 by Jean Foucault, uses a large iron ball as the bob, connected to a 200-foot (61-meter) line. The arc of a Foucault pendulum seems to rotate very slowly as the ball swings back and forth. Actually it is not that the arc is rotating, but rather the earth is rotating under the arc of the pendulum. If one were able to look at the pendulum from a fixed point in space far away from the earth, one would see that the direction of the arc remains fixed in space but the earth makes one rotation under the arc each 24 hours. If a circle below a Foucault pendulum is marked in hours and minutes, the pendulum will give the time.   P.F.D.

SEE ALSO: CLOCKS, GALILEO, GRAVITY

Peneplain

Peneplain A peneplain is a land surface worn nearly flat by EROSION. Broad valleys with gentle slopes are characteristic features. Streams that cross a peneplain deposit SEDIMENT rather than erode the land; meanders are common. A lowland is the main landform, with more-resistant rocks rising above the general land level.

Penguin

Penguin The penguin is a large bird, often as tall as 4 feet (1.2 meters). It cannot fly but swims well. It can also stand erect and walk well.

The short tail, webbed feet and scale-like feathers help to make the penguin a fast swimmer. It propels itself with its wings both underwater and on the surface, using its legs as a rudder. Even its eyes are adapted for underwater vision. It feeds on fish and mollusks.

Penguin range in color from black and white to bluish gray and some kinds have bright orange or yellow markings. It molts all at once and the feathers grow back in about 14 days.

All but one of the 15 species of penguin live in the cold seas of the Southern Hemisphere. They are found on islands off Africa, Australia, New Zealand, in the Arctic Ocean, and on Antarctica. One col-

ony of about 250 birds lives on the Galapagos Islands, near the equator.

The penguin courtship begins early in the winter. Birds tend to keep the same mates year after year and return to the same nesting grounds. Some species nest in holes and under rocks and others on the surface. Often the males are left to incubate the eggs, not eating for weeks as they do. Since penguins live closely together in colonies, the adults often share the care and feeding of the young. The adults of some species swim out for food, and, as they return, feed the first and hungriest babies they find. In other species, the adults carefully find their own young. The fledglings reach down their parents' throats for partly digested food. In an Emperor penguin colony, it is not unusual to see a huge nursery of young birds guarded by one adult male. The young require several months to grow to full adult size.   E. R. B.

Penicillin

Penicillin Penicillin was the first ANTIBIOTIC to be used successfully in the treatment of bacterial infections. Antibiotics are substances which are formed by living organisms. They are produced by MOLDS, soil organisms, and BACTERIA. Antibiotics interfere seriously with the organisms which produce disease. Penicillin has been used to treat many diseases that once were a great threat to life.

In 1928, SIR ALEXANDER FLEMING made a very great discovery. He found that a simple mold could destroy disease-producing bacteria. He noticed that a large colony

Laboratory-grown penicillium mold
Abbott Laboratories

of *staphylococcus* bacteria became transparent and hence dead, when they grew near a contaminating mold. This observation was the key to the discovery.

Fleming cultivated the mold in liquid broth, and noticed that during growth a substance was formed which inhibited the growth of some organisms. He called this penicillin, for the mold was *Penicillium notatum.*

Fleming then showed by experimentation that the extract containing penicillin was not poisonous to animals.

Since penicillin is a product of a mold, other species of molds were investigated for the presence of substances with similar properties. Thus a large number of antibiotic agents were discovered.

At present, several different forms of penicillin are known, and have been synthesized in the laboratory.   J. R. S.
SEE ALSO: BACTERIOLOGY

Peninsula (puh-NINN-suh-luh) A peninsula is almost an island. It juts out from a larger land mass. The state of Florida is a good example, as are Baja California and the "boot" of Italy. Many peninsulas have very broad bases where they connect with the continent.

Penis see Reproductive systems

Pennsylvanian see Geologic time table, Paleozoic Era

Penumbra Penumbra is the lighter or outer portion of a shadow. The term is mainly used to describe an ECLIPSE of either the sun or the moon. In a partial *solar* eclipse, the observer is positioned in the penumbra of the moon's shadow and sees only a portion of the sun blocked out. During a partial *lunar*

eclipse, the moon enters the penumbra of the earth's shadow.

Peony (PEE-uh-nee) The peony is one of the showiest of garden flowers. The kind most popular is a hybrid of the *common peony* of Europe and the *Chinese peony.*

Peonies belong to the *crowfoot,* or *buttercup,* family. It is a herbaceous PERENNIAL that reaches a height of about 3 feet (.9 meter). The flowers usually appear during June. They have single or double blooms ranging in color from white to red to purple. The leaves possess deep grooves or divisions. The fleshy roots store food material for new growth each year. The stem has a red to green color. When peony bushes are separated and transplanted to a new location, flowers will not appear for a year or two while the plant rests.

Some peonies have woody stems and are called *tree peonies.* They grow about 5 feet (1.5 meters) tall with many branches and a great number of blossoms. The woody tree peonies are native to Pacific coastal areas of Asia and North America.   H.J.C.
SEE ALSO: HYBRIDIZATION

Peperomia (peh-puh-ROME-yuh) Peperomia is a tropical plant raised for its attractive leaves. The leaves are a bright, shiny green with interesting markings and colors. Some leaves have brown, purple, or dark red markings, and others have light colored stripes between the veins.

Peperomia comes from the moist forests of Brazil. It is a member of the PEPPER family. *Peperomia* is a Greek word meaning "pepper-like." It is an annual or perennial herb, depending on the variety.

Peperomia is a small-growing plant used in greenhouses, as a pot plant, or in hanging baskets. It should be shaded in summer, and

Double peony

F. A. Blashfield

Peperomia

Pepper, the spice   **Red, or chili, pepper**   **Green and red pepper**

requires lots of moisture and regular applications of liquid fertilizer.

The plants of this group are succulent with thick, fleshy, slightly oval leaves, 3 to 6 inches (7.6 to 15.2 centimeters) long. Its tiny flowers are crowded on a dense, slender, usually curving spike.   M.R.L.
SEE ALSO: PLANTS, SUCCULENT

Pepper Pepper is the name for several plants and products. The best known is black pepper, a spice for flavoring food. It comes from a tropical vine native to the East Indies, Thailand and India. Twice a year the vine bears fruit in the form of green berries, which turn red. They are picked, dried in the sun and turn black. Then they are ground into fine, black pepper powder. The whole berries are called *peppercorns*. To get the best flavor, the peppercorns should be ground in a pepper mill at the time they are to be used.

White pepper is ground from the same ripe berries, after the dark outer rind has been removed.

Red pepper, not related to either black or white, is the dried, crushed pods of a large variety of hot chilies.

Green and *red* peppers found in vegetable markets are from entirely different plants, and their history has always been confused with the common table spice. They are called *sweet* or *bell peppers* and are berry-like fruits, related to the tomato and used fresh or cooked in salads, soups, and stews. The red bell pepper is simply the ripened green bell pepper. They were first found in the West Indies by a botanist of the Columbus expedition, who took samples back to Europe with him.   J. K. K.
SEE ALSO: CAYENNE, PAPRIKA, PIMENTO

Peppermint A favorite member of the MINT family, peppermint is an HERB used for medicines, perfumes, soaps, and for flavoring foods and candy.

There are two common varieties of peppermint, black and white. The black has dark green leaves, square stems, and purple blossoms tinged with red at the tips of long spikes. The white is a similar plant but shorter and with lighter green leaves. The oil taken from the leaves of the white peppermint is the best quality.   J. K. K.

Pepsin see Enzymes

Peptic ulcer see Ulcer

Perception see Eye

Perch Darters, walleyed pike, and perch are all in the perch family. They are shallow-water fish and are found all over the world in lakes, slow-moving rivers, and ponds. They feed on eggs, larvae, insects, and other fish.

All perch have two anal spines rather than three. The soft and spiny parts of the dorsal fin are separated. The common yellow perch has six to nine black bars on the sides of its body. Ventral and anal fins are orange. They are small fish, 1 to 5 inches (2.5 to 38.1 centimeters) long; a fish weighing about a pound (.5 kilogram) is considered large.

Perch lay eggs in long strings, sometimes over 10,000 in a string that attaches to vegetation. Young do not develop the yellow color until they are around 4½ inches (11.4 centimeters) long.   J.C.K.
SEE ALSO: FISH, PISCES

Yellow perch

Chicago Natural History Museum

Some perfume flowers—(from left) lavender, jasmine, violets

Percussion (per-KUHSH-uhn) Percussion is the act of striking an object with a sharp, quick blow. The blow may be delivered by the hand or some instrument especially designed for the purpose of striking the object.

More commonly, percussion is related to the production of musical tones or rhythms. Many musical instruments employ the principles of percussion. The *drum* is considered a percussion instrument and is used for keeping the tempo or "beat" of the music. *Cymbals, tambourines,* and *castanets* are other examples of the same type of percussion instrument. The *piano* and *xylophone* are percussion instruments also, but they are capable of producing melodies as well as keeping the tempo.

Along more purely scientific lines, percussion is used to describe a point on an object such as a PENDULUM. When a blow is delivered to exactly that point, it will cause rotation only around the place of suspension. This point is known as the *center of percussion.* An example of this effect is shown by a baseball and a bat. If the batter hits the ball directly on the center of percussion, there will be no shock transmitted to the batter's hands as would be the case if the ball were hit any other place on the bat. A. E. L.

SEE ALSO: MUSICAL INSTRUMENTS

Perennial (puh-RENN-ee-uhl) A perennial is a plant that lives longer than two years. A BIENNIAL lives two years. An ANNUAL lives one growing season.

Woody perennials include trees and shrubs. They have stems that live for many years. Each year, a new season's growth is added and the stem increases in diameter. Most woody perennials lose only their leaves after the growing season, and *evergreens* retain even their leaves or needles, sometimes for three years. *Herbaceous perennials* have stems that die down to the ground after the growing season. Plants such as RHUBARB, LILY, ASPARAGUS, and many GRASSES live through the winter and use stored food from underground parts, such as tubers, rootstocks, and bulbs, to produce new shoots that grow the following season. M. R. L.

SEE ALSO: ANGIOSPERMS, ANNUAL RING, BULB, TUBER

Perfume (PURR-fyoom) Perfume is a substance with a pleasing odor. It is made by blending oils, alcohol, and other materials.

Perfume has been in use since ancient times. In ancient Egypt, it was considered a symbol of immortality and was often placed in the tombs of the Pharaohs. The Bible frequently refers to the use of perfume. Perfume has grown in popularity through the ages, and is a favorite with women who like its good scent on their skin and clothing. It is used in soaps, shaving lotions, shampoos, cosmetics, and hundreds of other products.

The finest perfumes are expensive because of the high cost of the essential oils and fixatives used in their preparation. They are made in nearly all countries, but France is considered the leader of the perfume industry. Fragrant flowers such as lavender, carnations, jasmine, orange blossoms, and violets are raised in France and made into famous French perfumes. The finest rose perfume is made in Bulgaria. Most of the spice scents come from tropical regions.

Gland cells in the nectaries of flowers produce fragrant oils. These oils, or *attars,* are the essential oils that are blended with other ingredients to make perfumes. The essential oils are removed from flowers either by steam DISTILLATION; by allowing lard to absorb the oil; or by dissolving the flower oils with petroleum ether. It takes many thousands of pounds of flowers to produce an ounce of essential oil. This is one reason for the high cost of perfumes.

Fixatives are used in perfumes to make the scent last and to blend the many separate odors into one fine scent. Animal products such as ambergris, civet, and musk are fixatives. They must be properly treated, aged, and blended before use. Natural fixatives are very expensive and add greatly to the cost of perfume. Synthetic musk has been successfully made and used. M. R. L.

Pericardium The pericardium is the closed membranous sac which envelops the HEART of vertebrates and some other animals. It holds the clear, serous liquid with which the heart is bathed. It consists of an outer and inner coat.

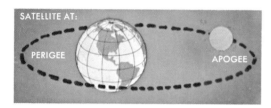

Perigee The point in the orbit of a revolving satellite closest to the body around which it revolves is the *perigee*. Earth reaches its perigee each year on January 3, when it is 91½ million miles (147¼ million kilometers) from the sun. Both natural and man-made satellites have curved, not circular, orbits. Each has a perigee in its orbit.

SEE ALSO: APOGEE, ORBITAL SYSTEMS

Period see Geologic time table

Periodic table see Elements, Mendeleev's Periodic Table

Peripatus (puhr-RIP-uh-tuss) These shy little animals look like a caterpillar because they have short, stubby legs and a wrinkled body. But they are not insects. They have a long, soft, body and are often called "walking worms". But they are not worms.

These animals are not easy to find. They live in warm countries, like Africa and South America. Although all of them live on land, they must live in a damp place. They find shelter under stones, logs and tree roots in wet, tropical forests and come out only at night or during a rain.

Peripatus feeds upon decaying vegetation, insects, especially termites, worms, and snails.

Buchsbaum
Peripatus resembles a worm with legs

The peripatus seems to feed only upon dead animals. It is able to catch insects, termites and worms in a very interesting way. From two large salivary glands on its head, it spits out a sticky secretion like rubber cement. As this secretion dries, it entangles the prey.

Scientists often place the peripatus in a separate phylum with the name *Onychophora,* meaning "claw bearer." Although there are only about eighty different species, these animals were the first to have a true leg. From 14 to 40 pairs of fleshy legs turn downward and lift the animal off the ground. The peripatus provides a missing link between the segmented worms (annelids) and the jointed-legged arthropods.

Like the annelids, they have a segmented head, fleshy, unjointed legs, and a similar excretory system. Like the arthropods, they have feet with curved claws, and a well-developed head which bears two long antennae. Like the insects, they breathe by means of tracheal tubes.

The male peripatus has three or four fewer legs than does the female. Most females retain the embryos inside their bodies until they are ready to be born. Since pregnancy for the peripatus lasts for over a year, the female may carry two litters of young at the same time. At birth, the peripatus is about .5 inch (1.3 centimeters) long. However, it grows to a length of about 5 inches (12.7 centimeters).   E.P.L.

SEE ALSO: ANIMALS, CLASSIFICATION OF; ANNELIDA; ARTHROPODA; EVOLUTION

Periscope (PAIR-uh-skope) A periscope is an OPTICAL INSTRUMENT which enables a person to obtain a view otherwise impossible to see. Peri-

✳ **THINGS TO DO**

MAKING A PERISCOPE   1″ = 2.5 cm.   1′ = .3 m.

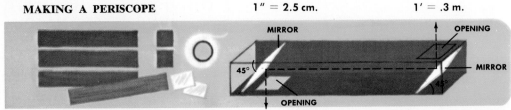

If you are too short to see over people's heads in a crowd then make this instrument. It will also enable you to peek around corners without your being noticed.

1 Cut four strips of balsa wood measuring three inches by one foot. These will form the sides of the tube. Cut two more pieces measuring three by three inches for the ends.

2 Cut out a two-inch square near the end of two side strips. Tape pocket mirrors at a 45 degree angle to the two sides with holes. Follow the illustration carefully. Tape the remaining sides, the top and bottom pieces to form a completely closed box.

3 It is now ready for use. Hold the tube upright and look through the bottom opening. Since light travels in straight lines the mirrors will reflect the object down to your eyes.

scopes allow a SUBMARINE crew to survey objects on the surface of the water. A simple periscope can be made by mounting two mirrors on an angle within a tube or a narrow box. A person can look around a corner or over a fence with this homemade periscope.

A submarine periscope consists of a long, stainless steel or bronze tube. The optical lenses and prisms are sealed at the top by a glass window so they are watertight. When the periscope is raised above the surface of the water, light enters through the window. The light, striking a right-angle prism at the top, is totally reflected downward through several lenses to a second prism or a mirror. At this level the light is again totally reflected to the eyepiece, and thus to the observer.

Periscopes are also used for other military purposes. Warships and gun turrets may contain range-finding periscopes designed to protect the operator from enemy fire. Tanks use periscopes, as do foot soldiers in trenches.

Periscopes are employed to observe radioactive materials. This is one way scientists can see over or through protective walls. Scientists can examine the inside of the stomach with a periscope-type instrument called the *gastroscope*.   P. F. D.

SEE ALSO: LENS, MAN-MADE; PRISM; TELESCOPE

Peristalsis (per-uh-STAL-siss) Peristalsis is a type of movement, occurring in the hollow organs of animals, which causes the contents of the organ to be pushed out. Peristalsis occurs when the *circular* and *longitudinal muscle fibers* of the organ contract in rhythm. It occurs in circulatory, reproductive, and excretory systems but is most apparent in the digestive tract, where food is churned, mixed, and moved by peristalsis.

Circular fiber contraction makes the organ narrower and longer, while longitudinal fiber contraction makes it wider and shorter. The contractions begin at the top and run consecutively down the organ. If peristalsis is reversed in the upper digestive tract, vomiting occurs.   J. K. L.

SEE ALSO: DIGESTIVE SYSTEM

Peritoneum (pair-ih-tah-NEE-um) The peritoneum is a smooth, paper-thin, fibrous membrane that lines the inside of the ABDOMEN. It consists of two layers. The outer or *parietal* layer starts at the DIAPHRAGM and runs down the inside of the abdominal wall into the pelvis. There it turns backward and becomes the inner or *visceral* layer.

SEE ALSO: ABDOMEN, PERITONITIS, TYPHOID FEVER

Peritonitis (Per-uh-tuh-NYE-tiss)

Peritonitis is an inflammation of the PERITONEUM, the *serous* membrane that lines the abdominal cavity from the DIAPHRAGM to the pelvis, enveloping the intestines, stomach, and front of the liver.

If the APPENDIX should burst because of infection, bacteria could enter the peritoneal cavity and cause peritonitis. Other common causes of the disease are rupture of a stomach ulcer, tuberculosis of the bowel, or perforation by a bullet or stab wound. It is a very serious condition in which the abdomen becomes painful and distended. Surgery may be required. The condition is accompanied by profuse perspiration, chills and fever.

Treating peritonitis involves the use of large quantities of antibiotics given intravenously, sometimes for several weeks. This prevents *septicemia* (blood poisoning or bacteria in the blood), shock, and/or death. If an abscess is formed, surgery is sometimes performed to drain it. Peritonitis, before antibiotics, was often fatal. Even now it is a very serious disease, best prevented instead of treated. B.M.H./E.S.S.

Periwinkle (animal)

The periwinkle is a little SNAIL with a thick spiral shell. The shell is yellow, black, brown, or red with dark bands.

Periwinkles can be eaten and are used as fish bait. They are common in European waters and are now found on the Atlantic coast.

The periwinkle's head sticks out of the shell and its eyes are at the end of tentacles. When the animal moves, it swings from side to side on a foot that is divided lengthwise.

J. W. Thompson
The periwinkle is smaller than a man's thumb

The snail's tongue is twice as long as its body. The periwinkle clings to rocks where it lays its eggs and eats plants. P. G. B.

Periwinkle (plant) see Vinca

Permafrost

Permafrost is a permanently frozen subsoil. It occurs in about one-fourth of the earth's land surface. It is generally found in Arctic regions where short summers do not warm the soil enough to melt trapped water below.

Permafrost is continuous throughout the Arctic and can become hundreds of feet or meters thick in the high polar regions. It thins out further away from the poles until it disappears in the lower latitudes. Permafrost begins when the total heat balance of the soil produces temperatures continuously below 32 ° F. (0° C.) for a period of several years. P.P.S.

Permeability (per-mee-uh-BILL-uh-tee)

Permeability is a measure of how easily fluids can penetrate and flow through a solid. Solids are permeable because they have networks of pore spaces through which fluids can flow.

Permeability is an important property of building materials and textiles. The permeability of sedimentary rocks like sandstone and limestone, through which flow water and oil into wells, has been the most carefully studied.

Magnetic permeability is a property of a substance which tells how much it becomes magnetized when placed in a magnetic field. The higher the magnetic permeability of a substance, the more highly magnetized it becomes when placed in a magnetic field.

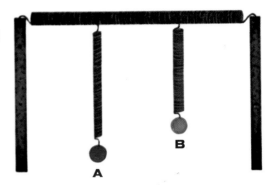

Permeability is also a property of semi-permeable membranes. In this case, permeability is a measure of how rapidly a substance on one side of the membrane can diffuse through the membrane to the other side. The membranes around plant and animal cells are *selectively permeable*. These membranes will allow certain ions to pass through but will not permit other ions to pass.   E. R. B.

SEE ALSO: MAGNETS, OSMOSIS

Peroxide see Oxygen

Perpendicular Perpendicular means exactly upright or at right angles to a line. A line perpendicular to another line or plane forms a 90 degree angle with that line or plane.

Perpetual motion machine This is a type of machine that, once started, should run forever without any additional energy being supplied to it from an outside source. This *ideal* machine could supply energy to run other pieces of equipment without having any energy requirement of its own. Such a machine is only theoretically possible.

The scientific view today is that a real perpetual motion machine is a practical impossibility. The reasoning is as follows.

Any machine starts to operate when supplied with some definite amount of energy of the proper type (for which the machine was designed) and of the proper "energy order-level." Examples of high-level energy sources are: the mechanical motions of an engine drive rod; a steady current of electricity; and a hot object sending its heat into a colder object (molecular motion). The cold object, in the latter example, may be considered as a low-level energy source.

As the machine starts up, the moving parts rub together and wear away. Thus they waste some of the original high-level motion and spread it about as worn machine fragments and low-level heat. In short, friction and heat loss are the two ever-present conquerors of perfect use of energy and thus of perpetual motion. The *second law of thermodynamics* states that the heat in a material cannot be completely changed into mechanical energy—except if the machine could work at absolute zero ($-460°$ F., $-273.1°$ C.). ABSOLUTE ZERO temperature has never been reached.

The planets and natural satellites, such as the moon, do seem to travel about their central bodies perpetually, for they move in the near-vacuum of space and undergo little or no friction. The main friction-like forces on satellites are those made by space debris—meteors or comets. Such debris—or large-sized collisions—might sometime end the perpetual motion of even these bodies.

One of the many proposed perpetual motion machines is that sketched above. It has three springs, one of which is supported by two upright rods. The other two have metal spheres at their lower ends.

The system is started by introducing energy into sphere A; that is, it is set to vibrating up and down. Eventually sphere B will vibrate and A will come to rest.

This process will repeat itself for quite some time. Then why will it fail in perpetual motion? There will always be some air friction; and even in a vacuum, there will also be the internal friction and heat loss of the molecules in the springs themselves. Without adding more outside energy then, this machine will finally run down.

The perpetual motion idea has been valuable since it has led men to build better machines—with better lubrication and finer parts, such as ball bearings.   A. E. L.

Perrin, Jean Baptiste (1870-1942) Jean Baptiste Perrin, an important French scientist, won the 1926 NOBEL PRIZE for physics. He pioneered in research on atomic structure.

Perrin won the Nobel Prize for his studies on the discontinuous structure of matter and the equilibrium of sedimentation. He also did research on atomic structure around the turn of the century. In the late

Perseus

1800s Perrin experimented with CATHODE RAYS and discovered a negative charge associated with them. Further investigations of cathode rays by other scientists led to the discovery of the electron. A.J.H.

Perseus Perseus is a beautiful group of stars in the Milky Way. The CONSTELLATION was named for a mythical Greek hero, the son of Zeus, who beheaded the wicked Medusa. A glance from Medusa would have turned him to stone, but he was aided by Mercury and Minerva. The ancient Greeks believed the constellation to be Perseus holding the severed head of Medusa.

Though not easy to find, Perseus is visible with a small telescope. It is seen in the northern sky in December and January, and reaches from Cassiopeia to Taurus. The star *Algol,* visible to the naked eye, is actually a double star. The light shed by Algol is variable, caused by the revolving of the dim STAR around the bright star every three days, producing a partial eclipse.

A telescope will reveal many variously colored star clusters in the constellation. About August 10th the famous meteor shower, the *Perseids,* can be seen. C. L. K.

Persimmon The persimmon tree has pale orange fruits. They are juicy berries about 2 inches (5 centimeters) in diameter. The leaves are long and narrow. The flowers are white. Persimmons belong to the EBONY family.

The American persimmon grows from 50 to 100 feet (15.2 to 30.5 meters) tall, has a spreading, rounded head, and drooping branches. The plum-like fruits are colored yellow and pink. The taste of the persimmon is mouth-puckering until fully ripe.

The Japanese persimmon or *kaki* is a smaller tree, rarely reaching more than 40 feet (12.2 meters) in height. Its fruit is larger and redder than that of the American persimmon. The fruit of the Japanese persimmon is the one most frequently marketed. J.K.K.

Persistence of vision Persistence of vision is the ability of human eyes to retain an image of what they have just seen for a short period of time after the object has disappeared from sight. A person can "see" a light for a second or two after the light has been turned off.

If an electric light bulb is placed behind an electric fan moving at high speed, the light seems to shine continuously although the fan blades are covering it for short intervals. This persistence of vision explains why still pictures shown rapidly appear to move. Motion pictures are actually numerous still pictures shown so rapidly that they seem to blend into one continuous moving picture. E. R. B.
SEE ALSO: MOTION PICTURES

Perspective Perspective is the science or art of drawing an object on a flat or curved surface so that the object appears to have depth and be at a distant point from an observer. The visual rays from the object appear to converge at the observer's eye.
SEE: EYE; EYE, BINOCULAR; LENS, MAN-MADE

Perspiration see Sweat glands

Perutz, Max F. (1914-) The 1962 NOBEL PRIZE for chemistry was won by Max Perutz and John Kendrew. Perutz was able to determine the molecular structure of *hemoglobin.*

Hemoglobin is an important compound in oxygen transporting in many biological systems. It is a very large and complex molecule. Perutz used X-ray crystallography in his research. He combined this tech-

Petrel

nique with the "heavy atom" method. Hemoglobin crystals were labeled with mercury. Their X-ray diffraction patterns were compared with those of unlabeled hemoglobin. These techniques can be used to determine structures of other complex protein molecules. A.J.H.

Petrel The petrel is a bird about the size of a MARTIN. It lives on the open sea, returning to shore to nest. One egg is laid; young are hatched covered with gray down. Adults are dark with white rumps and webbed feet.

SEE ALSO: FALCON

Petrifaction (pet-ruh-FACK-shun) Petrifaction is the process in which materials such as wood become rock formations. This happens through a replacement of the original substance by minerals of various types. The best known examples are the Petrified Forests found in Arizona. These are classified as a kind of FOSSIL.

SEE ALSO: PALEONTOLOGY

Petroleum (puh-TROW-lee-uhm) Petroleum, or crude mineral oil, was formed during the time when ancient, warm, inland seas covered much of the area that is land today. These warm seas contained vast numbers of plants and animals that eventually died, sank to the sea floor, and were later covered by sediments. It was from the remains of these organic fossils that petroleum was formed.

The formation of petroleum deposits required thousands of years. Later movements within the earth's crust resulted in the upward folding of these deposits, and they were brought closer to the surface of the earth. Movement within the earth's crust often resulted in the trapping of large pockets, or reservoirs, of natural gas, crude oil, and salt

water. Large quantities of petroleum are also trapped in tar sands and oil shales. Considerable research toward the recovery of this petroleum is under way.

The most important early product of oil was *kerosene,* and the lighter *gasoline,* which would explode in kerosene lamps, was thrown away. Today, the chief products are NATURAL GAS, gasoline, kerosene, lubricating oil, FUEL oils, asphalts, and oil coke.

The production of oil in the United States is steadily decreasing. However, the uses of oil in the United States are increasing. The result is that the United States must import millions of gallons of petroleum products each year.

Due to worldwide demand, petroleum is at the center of many heated political, economic, and ecological problems. Oil was a significant issue in the 1991 Gulf War. Following their invasion of the oil-rich nation of Kuwait, Iraqi soldiers were driven out by a military counterattack led by U.S. forces. The retreating Iraqis set fire to more than seven hundred oil wells, creating an economic and ecological nightmare. Workers from sixteen nations worked for eight months to put out the fires, at a cost of about two billion dollars. A number of soldiers and oil workers have reported health problems that may be the result of breathing the highly polluted air around the burning wells.

Mishaps aboard huge supertankers, ships that carry vast quantities of petroleum, also create environmental problems. Tremendous damage to the coast of Alaska occurred when the *Exxon Valdez* supertanker ran aground in 1991 and dumped nearly 11 million gallons (more than 41 million liters) of oil into Prince William Sound. Oil spills in other parts of the world have released as much as five times more oil as the *Exxon Valdez* tragedy.

In the early 1990s, nations with the largest known reserves of petroleum were Saudi Arabia, Iraq, Kuwait, and Venezuela. Some nations, such as the U.S., Canada, and England, were pumping oil at a rate that would probably lead to internal shortages in just a few years.

Scientists believe that about one-third of the petroleum that exists in the world has already been used. With demand for oil increasing, international tensions and ecological concerns are bound to increase in the future. H.S.G./A.J.H./J.H.

SEE ALSO: ENERGY CRISIS, FOSSIL FUELS, GREENHOUSE EFFECT, OIL WELL

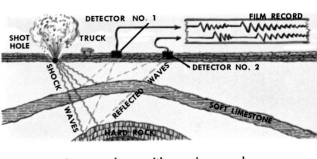

Locating petroleum with a seismograph

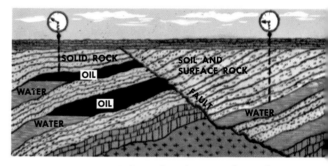

In giant oil fractionating towers, crude oil is made into high-octane gasoline

American Oil Co.

The gravimeter can help in locating petroleum deposits. When used over a fault, as shown above, gravity registers stronger on the raised side of the fault as dense rock is closest there. Below is shown the gravimeter registering less gravitational pull as it is used over a salt dome, because salt is lighter than surrounding rock

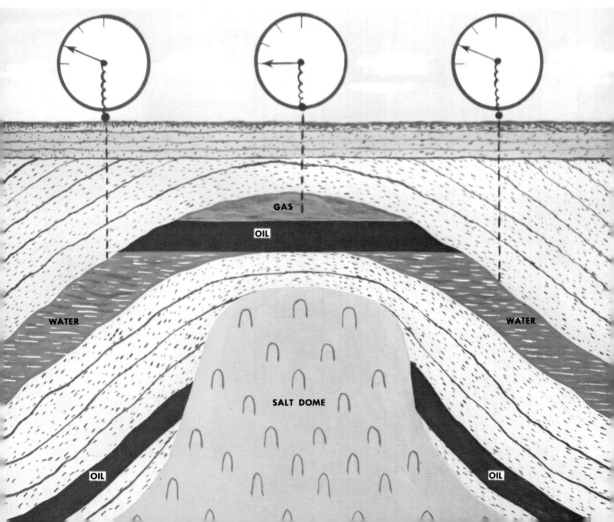

Petroleum jelly Petroleum jelly, or *petrolatum,* is a semi-solid substance obtained by refining the greases which result from the distillation of PETRO-LEUM. It is used as a protective dressing, a base for ointments, a lubricant for metals, and a leather-softener.

Petrology see Rocks

Helen J. Challand

Pink petunias

Petunia Some of these flowering HERBS are ANNUAL, living for only one year. Other kinds, PERENNIALS, continue growing for several years. The velvety, funnel-shaped FLOWERS vary in color from white to pink, red, violet, or blue. LEAVES are hairy and dark green. They are alternate on the stems.

There are many species of petunia. Some dwarf varieties are very short, while other species are over 2 feet (.6 meter) high. Stems may be upright or sprawling. Petunia blossoms are "perfect," having both male and female parts in the same flower. Hybrids have recently been developed that have petals that are doubled, fringed, striped, or marked with a five-pointed star. Each flower has five stamens and one pistil composed of two carpels. The ovary matures into a capsule FRUIT.

Petunias belong to the nightshade or Solanaceae family.   H.J.C.

Pewter Antique pewter was an ALLOY of tin and lead. Because lead is highly poisonous, modern pewter is an alloy of tin, antimony, and copper. It is used primarily for making utensils.

SEE ALSO: METAL

pH acids Acids contain hydrogen ions. pH is a scale that tells the concentration of hydrogen ions. A hydrogen ion is an atom of hydrogen without its electron.

pH is defined as the negative log of the hydrogen ion concentration. The hydrogen ion concentration must be expressed in *moles* of hydrogen ions per liter of solvent. A pH between 1 and 7 is an *acid* solution. A pH between 7 and 14 is a *basic* solution. A pH of 7 is a *neutral* solution.   A.J.H.

Pharmacology (fahr-muh-KAHL-uh-jee) Pharmacology is the science that deals with the action of medicines and other chemicals on animals and man. It is different from *pharmacy,* which is the preparing and mixing of medicines of known action.

Pharmacology is a young science. It recently has become important not only to doctors and druggists but also to research biologists studying newly produced chemicals.

Many nineteenth-century biochemists helped build this science of drug action. Two of the most prominent contributors were Francis Magendie and Otto Schmiederberg.

In ancient times and until the last century, knowledge of how DRUGS cure disease was unreliable. Superstition and magic influenced early alchemists and herb collectors. They wrote thick "books of medicines" called *pharmacopoeias,* and these books recommended many drugs that were either worthless or harmful, when examined by the standards of modern pharmacology. For example, powdered dandelion root was listed in pharmacopoeia books as a "cure for colds, kidney stones, and deep fevers."

However, medicinal plants, such as DIGITALIS, the medieval herb extract of foxglove plants, have been shown to contain a number of chemicals useful in treating certain types of heart disease. An old herb discovery of the South American Indians—the bark of the cinchona tree containing quinine—has been used for centuries to treat MALARIA. During World War II, phar-

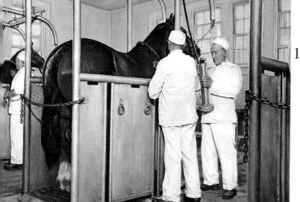

The development of biological serums started about 1894 with the use of diphtheria toxin

About 1920, Fourneau of France produced many compounds to fight specific diseases

macologists and medical men developed a drug called *Atabrine,* an improvement over quinine. During the Korean War, pharmacologists developed *chloroquine,* a further improvement.

THE BRANCHES OF PHARMACOLOGY

Four branches of the science are recognized: *pharmacodynamics* deals with finding how chemicals act on men's bodies, or first on those of laboratory animals.

Chemotherapy includes two studies: how drug chemicals can destroy invading germs and how normal health can be restored to unbalanced organs and glands. The *antibiotic* medicines, such as PENICILLIN and sulfa, are useful in treating certain bacterial infections in humans. Some antibiotics *(bacteriocidal)* act directly upon bacteria to kill them. Others *(bacteriostatic)* prevent bacteria from multiplying. Pharmacology made possible the discovery of INSULIN in 1921, a lifesaving drug for use in DIABETES. It is given by injection. Newly developed pills help control mild diabetes.

Clinical pharmacology is practiced by research doctors in hospital clinics. After the *pharmacodynamic* action of a new drug has been determined, that chemical becomes ready for testing on volunteer patients. Clinical trial makes it possible to determine the effects of different drugs on different diseases.

Toxicology is the fourth branch of drug research. Certain drugs and chemicals are poisonous (toxic) to living cells. The toxicologist determines which are harmful and tries to develop antidotes. For example, exposure to lead causes lead poisoning, but a certain chemical (EDTA) can draw excess lead from the body. This chemical in turn has its own toxic effects.

SCIENTIFIC DOSAGES

Doctors have long been concerned about how to find the correct dose of a medicine. The scientist first tests the drug and records all doses.

Suppose that an entirely new chemical with some curative effect is discovered. The drug scientist first tests and records all the doses which were administered to laboratory animals and later to human volunteers. Then he reports to drug manufacturers and physicians just what the best doses and effects are. To do this, he reports the *effective dose response* (ED), meaning that dose required to produce one-half (50%) of its observed curing effect. For example, ASPIRIN to relieve a fever due to a cold might be reported: "Aspirin, antifebrile, ED_{50} dose 2.5 grains every 2 hours, per 150-pound (68-kilogram) adult body weight." The full dose for an adult this size would be 5 grains every two hours, or, as commonly given, 10 grains (two tablets) every four hours.

METHODS OF DRUG STUDY

Good drug-action research usually follows certain accepted methods. Laboratory animals are given measured doses of a promising chemical. The bodily effects on the animals are accurately observed. Then perhaps certain bad effects of the drug cause the researcher to seek a related but slightly changed chemical. Often the researcher will go to a fellow organic chemist and ask for a similar chemical that has only one atom or a small molecular group of atoms changed. The new chemical is then given in measured doses to animals. This process may continue for many months until a drug is finally found that is satisfactory. It is then ready to be tried on volunteer clinical patients. In this very way, the old herbal drug, salicylic acid, was rejected for the much-improved acetylsalicylic acid, which is commonly known as ASPIRIN.

Since the discovery of penicillin, the synthesis of antibiotics has become vitally important

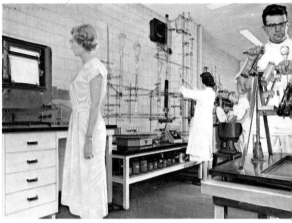

Continuous research in pharmaceuticals is the most important task of pharmacologists

NUCLEAR ENERGY ISOTOPES

Since World War II, pharmacology has found a powerful new discovery tool in radioisotopes. For example, radioiodine, a product of nuclear energy reactors, can be given by mouth to persons suffering from thyroid gland disease. The thyroid normally takes iodine out of the bloodstream and stores it. When the iodine is made radioactive, the amount of iodine absorbed by the gland can be "counted" by scanning with a GEIGER COUNTER. Similarly, radioactive iodine is excreted by the kidneys. By scanning over the kidney area, it can be determined if one or both kidneys are working properly.

Knowledge of the curing values of most medicines is owed to pharmacologists. It took ten years of study to extract the pure chemical penicillin from the crude, green mold discovered by Sir Alexander Fleming in 1928. Pharmacologists have also developed chemicals that will destroy the cells of some tumors. Some rare types of cancer have apparently been cured by these drugs. There is much work being done in this field, with great hope for more effective treatment in the future of cancer and other diseases. D.A.B./B.M.H.

SEE ALSO: MEDICINE, PHYSIOLOGY

Pharynx (FAIR-ingks) The pharynx is the section of the alimentary tract of some invertebrates connecting the mouth and esophagus. In vertebrates, it is the tube back of the nose and mouth where air crosses the path of food going to the esophagus.

SEE: ADENOID, DIGESTIVE SYSTEM, RESPIRATORY SYSTEM

Phases of the Moon see Earth; Moon, phases of

Pheasants These are large chicken-like birds. Both males and females have long arched tails. Females are mottled brown, but males are among the most colorful of all game birds. The head, neck, and rump are green, and the tail is barred with black.

Pheasants were successfully introduced into the United States from their native Asia in 1881. The ring-necked pheasant is a hybrid, a cross between the Chinese ring-necked variety and the English pheasant. Both the ring-necked and English pheasants (without a white neck ring) have since become naturalized.

These birds prefer a mixed habitat of brush, grass, and farmland. Large flocks may live in favorable areas. They fly well for short distances but usually run when disturbed. They nest in hollows, laying 5 to 16 greenish eggs. Young hatch in 22 days and fly in two weeks. J. C. K.

Male ring-necked pheasant

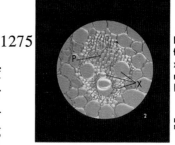

Phloem cells (P) carry food to plant cells; xylem (X) bring raw materials to the leaves.

Photomicrograph by National Teaching Aids, Inc.

Phenols The phenols are a group of organic compounds which have one or more HYDROXYL groups (OH) attached directly to an aromatic-ring system. The simplest is phenol (C_6H_5OH). They are used in disinfectants, plastics, and preservatives.
SEE: ORGANIC COMPOUNDS

Philodendron

Philodendron (fill-uh-DEN-drun) This HERB is a PERENNIAL, growing year after year. It thrives in tropical regions as a shrub. Some have short, erect stems; others are climbing vines.

Philodendron is grown for its attractive, large LEAVES. They may measure a few inches across and up to 3 feet (.9 meter) long and 2 feet (.6 meter) wide. The margins of the leaves may be lobed or smooth. The leaves are on long stalks. FLOWERS are small and inconspicuous. The ovary of each little flower matures into a BERRY fruit.

There are about 200 species of philodendron. They are in the Araceae, or arum, family.   H.J.C.

Phloem (FLO-emm) Inside a plant are groups of cells which carry on a particular job for the plant. Phloem makes up conducting tubes for the purpose of carrying the manufactured food to all parts of the plant. Phloem cells are found around the outside of XYLEM cells, the other kind of conducting tissue.

There are several kinds of cells in phloem. *Parenchyma* are large thin-walled storage cells. *Fibers* have thick walls to give the plant support and strength. *Sieve tubes* are elongated cells which retain their cytoplasm but lose their nuclei. They appear to need companion cells to help them function. The constant flow of solutions through the sieve cell may weaken the cross-walls and cause them to be perforated as a sieve.

Phloem tissue in trees makes up the inner part of the BARK. It is separated from the xylem tissue by a sheath of meristematic cells called *vascular cambium*. The cambium constantly divides and forms new phloem and xylem cells every year.   H. J. C.
SEE ALSO: PLANT TISSUES

Phlox (FLOCKS) Phlox is a flower that blooms all summer. The dwarf kind, no more than 6 inches (15.2 centimeters) tall, is found in many rock gardens. Another taller variety is used as a border herb. The blooms are commonly white or pink to purple.

This annual or perennial plant grows in a creeping manner or in an erect position. The leaves are alternate in arrangement with a smooth margin. The petals of the flower are fused to form a tube with the outer edges scalloped. The flower is perfect, meaning it has both male and female reproductive structures. Many hybrid varities now come fringed or star-shaped in a wide range of flaming colors.

In late fall or early spring, the mature plant should be dug up, the rootstock cut into several pieces and replanted over a wider area. This is referred to as multiplication of a flower bed by division. If phlox is permitted to reseed itself, the offspring will revert to the wild state.   H. J. C.

Phoebe see Peewee

Globe phlox

George J. Ball, Inc.

Phosphate Phosphate is the name given to the large series of chemical compounds which have as part of their formula a phosphate component. Of all the phosphate compounds, the most common are the ammonium, calcium and sodium salts of phosphoric acid. Any phosphate has PO₄ in its formula.

The most familiar phosphate compounds are inorganic and are used in large quantities in many industries. For example, *diammonium phosphate* is used as a fireproofing agent for textiles. *Monoammonium phosphate* is used in baking powders. *Monocalcium phosphate* is used as a dietary supplement in animal feeds, and the various sodium phosphates are used as laxatives, as buffering agents, and in detergent mixtures. M. S.
SEE ALSO: PHOSPHORUS, SALT

A lantern fish has organs which produce a phosphorescent glow

Phosphorescence (foss-for-ESS-sense) Phosphorescence is the condition in which certain organic or mineral matter and certain plants and animals give off light without the presence of heat. Also known as "afterglow," phosphorescence has been known to persist for a period of only a few seconds up to several days.

The scientific explanation of phosphorescence is that the substance absorbs radiant light energy which increases the energy of some of the electrons in the substance. When the electrons slowly return to their original state, they emit this extra energy in the form of light. If the radiation of a substance fades immediately after the light is stopped, the process is called *fluorescence*. If light continues, however, the process is called *phosphorescence*.

In ancient times, phosphorescence was, of course, seen and recorded as it appeared in nature. However, the earliest record of serious investigation and experimentation of this phenomenon comes from Bologna, Italy, where a cobbler and alchemist named Cascariola conducted extensive research with a barium compound.

The delayed luminescence of phosphorescence is the result of the object being subjected to an exciting light source. The time during which phosphorescence persists is known to decrease with an increase in temperature of the substance. The principles of phosphorescence are being applied in many new areas of research, using especially the highly phosphorescent ruby. D. A. B.
SEE ALSO: BULB, ELECTRIC

Phosphorus (FOHS-fuh-ruhs) Phosphorus is an element that is found in four different pure forms. Each form has different characteristics. Chemically it is a non-metal, related in its properties to the elements nitrogen and astatine.

Phosphorus was first isolated in 1669 by H. Brandt. It is the first element whose date of discovery is known. Brandt isolated phosphorus from animal urine. Phosphorus occurs in compound form in all fertile soils. It is necessary for all plant and animal life. In man it is found mainly in bones, teeth, muscles, and nervous tissues.

The most common form of phosphorus is a yellow waxy solid. This form is originally white, almost colorless, but turns yellow when exposed to light. Yellow phosphorus melts at 111.6° F. (44.2° C.), is extremely poisonous, and must be stored and cut underwater to prevent fire. When moist yellow phosphorus is exposed to air, it burns, forms phosphorus pentoxide, and glows from the heat generated. This glow, a chemical change, is unrelated to phosphorescence.

Red phosphorus, another form, is widely used in making safety MATCHES. Red phosphorus is produced by heating yellow phosphorus or exposing it to a bright light. It is not poisonous and must reach 500° F. (260° C.) to burn. It is used in making

A glow and heat are produced when phosphorus is exposed to air

bronzes, medicines, and in gas analysis.

There are other forms of phosphorus, named for their colors. Scarlet phosphorus is produced by dissolving yellow phosphorus in phosphorus tribromide and heating it to 357° F. (180.6° C.). The solid scarlet phosphorus then settles out. Violet phosphorus is produced by heating red phosphorus in contact with lead for 10 hours at 932° F. (500° C.). The phosphorus dissolves in the lead, upon cooling it separates as violet phosphorus.

Phosphorus for commercial purposes is obtained from rock PHOSPHATE, a phosphorus-rich mineral. Rock phosphate is purified by heating with sand and carbon. France and the United States are the largest producers of rock phosphate. Phosphorus is the eleventh most abundant element.

Phosphorus (symbol P) has an atomic number of 15. Its atomic weight is 30.9738.

J.K.L.

SEE ALSO: ATOM, ELEMENTS

Photochemical smog

Smog is the combination of smoke and fog. It is a complex mixture of gases, tiny solid particles, and small drops of liquids. Photochemical smog is produced when sunlight causes certain chemical reactions to occur.

The major parts of photochemical smog are related to combustion. Nitrogen oxides such as nitric oxide (NO) and nitrogen dioxide (NO_2) are present in smog. Hydrocarbons not completely burned during combustion are harmful compounds in photochemical smog.

Nitrogen dioxide reacts with sunlight to form nitrous oxide and atomic oxygen (O). Atomic oxygen is very active and can undergo many different reactions. It can react with O_2 to form *ozone,* with itself to form oxygen, or with hydrocarbons to form free radicals.

The complex hydrocarbons have high boiling points. Thus hydrocarbons act as nuclei for the formation of fog-type droplets. These droplets scatter light. Nitrogen dioxide is brownish in color and gives the smog a hazy, brownish color.

A.J.H.

SEE ALSO: AIR POLLUTION

Photochemistry

Photochemistry is the study of chemical changes involving light. It studies those processes in which light causes chemical changes. Also it studies the reverse processes in which chemicals react to emit light. *Photo* is from Greek meaning "light."

Photochemical processes of the first type are illustrated by what happens to a film when a picture is being taken, and by the whitening of dark-colored clothing or hair when exposed to sunlight. Examples of the second type are illustrated by the flashing of a firefly and the burning of candles or oil and gas lamps.

In nature, an important, photochemical change occurs in green plants. CHLOROPHYLL in the cells of green plants uses light to combine ordinary water and carbon dioxide chemically to make sugar. This photochemical process is called PHOTOSYNTHESIS.

Photochemistry is basic to making and developing of photographic FILM. A clear plastic film is coated with gelatine containing tiny grains of silver bromide. When the film is placed in a camera and light is focused on it through the shutter and lens, the silver bromide undergoes chemical changes in those spots where light strikes it. The grains in these spots are said to be *sensitized.* Chemical developers reduce the sensitized grains of silver bromide to metallic silver. Chemicals called *fixers* are next used to remove the silver bromide which was not sensitized.

BLUEPRINT paper is photochemically similar to film. But for blueprints, paper is coated with iron-ammonium citrate and ferrocyanides. Light changes these pale iron salts to deep blue ferric ferrocyanides. Developing an exposed print only requires washing it in water.

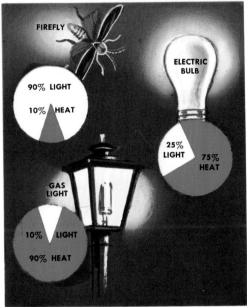

The firefly has a much more efficient photo-chemical process of light than does any of the light sources which man has been able to devise. Much less heat is produced for the amount of light given off

CHEMICAL PRODUCTION OF LIGHT

The oldest known photochemical change is that of burning fuels. Candles and gas or oil lamps are such light-giving devices. Even the best modern kerosene lamp is photo-chemically wasteful, since nine-tenths of the chemical energy in the original fuel is changed to heat and less than one-tenth to light. Even an electric light bulb wastes about 75 per cent of the original electrical energy as heat.

The reverse photochemical change has been difficult for man to produce. In nature, the firefly (lightning bug) has long been admired by scientists. In his laboratories, man has never yet found chemicals that give light matching the efficiency and coldness of the firefly's light.

Besides fireflies, many other living things perform photochemical feats. Fox fire is the glowing of decaying fallen logs, caused by bacteria that decompose the wood. Several kinds of sea animals produce light. The scallops (*Pectens*), clam-like animals that propel themselves by flapping their shells, have rows of phosphorescent eye spots lining the outer edges of their shells. When a scallop rests with its shell agape, small prey are lured into the scallop's vise-like shell body.   D. A. B.

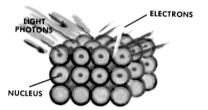

The outermost electrons of heavy metal atoms have weak binding force. They can be knocked loose by light and utilized as photoelectrical energy

Photoelectricity Photoelectricity is the study of how light and electricity work together. It has made possible the "electric eye" which automatically opens the doors of the supermarket, counts the number of articles made each hour in factories, and measures the brightness of distant stars. Even cameras now adjust themselves with its aid.

Light sometimes acts as though it were a stream of particles instead of waves. The brightness of the light is determined by the number of these particles, or PHOTONS, in the beam, while the energy of each individual particle determines what is called the *color* of the light.

Metals, like all matter, are made up of atoms. These, in turn, consist of a dense, positively-charged nucleus surrounded by a cloud of electrons. It is the electron's negative charge which binds it to the nucleus by electric-field attraction.

Since the atoms of most metals are relatively large, the outermost electrons are relatively far from the nucleus. As a result, the binding force upon these outer electrons is quite weak. When metal atoms are linked together to form a solid, the outer electrons can move freely anywhere in the solid and are called conduction electrons. If a photon of light is absorbed by a conduction electron, the additional energy may be enough to drive that electron out of the metal surface. When electrons are driven out continuously by light falling on a metal surface, a voltage can be applied between the surface and an electrode and the photoelectrons collected.

One of the major types of phototubes includes a semi-cylindrical CATHODE that has its inner surface coated with a light-sensitive alloy of cesium and silver. The anode is a

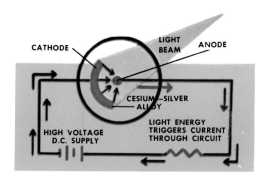

CATHODE — **LIGHT BEAM** — **ANODE**

CESIUM—SILVER ALLOY

LIGHT ENERGY TRIGGERS CURRENT THROUGH CIRCUIT

HIGH VOLTAGE D.C. SUPPLY

piece of wire arranged to collect any electrons driven out of the cathode.

As normally used, the cathode is connected to the negative side of a high voltage DC power supply, while the anode is connected to the positive side of the supply. A resistor is also connected in series with one of the electrodes. As long as the phototube is in the dark, it acts as an open circuit; no current can pass between its electrodes. However, when a beam of light strikes the sensitive cathode, the photons knock electrons from its surface. Being negatively charged, these electrons are strongly attracted to the positively-charged anode wire. These moving electrons thus form the current that flows around the entire circuit.

The picture below shows the simplified wiring diagram of an actual photoelectric relay, such as is widely used in industry. For simplicity the usual rectifier power supply has been replaced by batteries.

As long as the phototube remains in the dark, no current flows through the relay MAGNET coil. The spring holds the relay contacts open. But as soon as a light strikes the phototube, a current flows through the phototube and through the resistor. The voltage drop across the resistor causes the upper end of this resistor to become positive with respect to the lower end. This positive voltage overcomes the opposing effect of the battery. Thus the grid of the triode becomes positive and allows electrons to pass from its cathode to its plate and around through the relay coil. This current magnetizes the core of this coil and closes the contacts so that it starts any piece of apparatus connected to the terminals moving. This apparatus may be a door-opener motor or any common piece of electrical machinery.

When the light is removed, the phototube ceases to conduct. The triode grid again becomes negative; the current stops, and the magnet coil releases the contacts.

In recent years scientists have also found that light photons can change the electrical conductivity of a semiconductor junction. *Semiconductors* are such materials as SILICON and GERMANIUM and are used in transistors. By suitable chemical treatment during manufacture, silicon can be made in two

A broken light beam breaks current through a relay switch which falls to activate a motor circuit. The circuit will lower the drawbridge

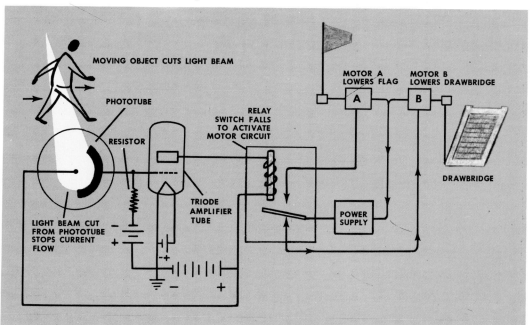

MOVING OBJECT CUTS LIGHT BEAM

PHOTOTUBE

RESISTOR

LIGHT BEAM CUT FROM PHOTOTUBE STOPS CURRENT FLOW

TRIODE AMPLIFIER TUBE

RELAY SWITCH FALLS TO ACTIVATE MOTOR CIRCUIT

MOTOR A LOWERS FLAG

MOTOR B LOWERS DRAWBRIDGE

A   B

POWER SUPPLY

DRAWBRIDGE

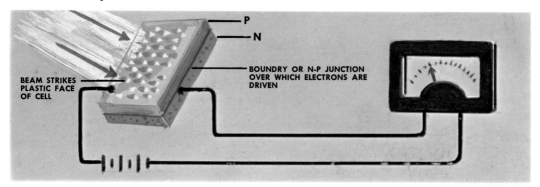

A system may be designed to operate a meter which measures the brightness of light

forms: (1) an "N material," and (2) a "P material." A single crystal of silicon is treated in both ways so that a boundary forms between them. This boundary is called a "P-N" semiconductor junction.

When a P-N semiconductor junction is connected, only a small current can flow across it in the dark, because the battery acts to prevent the free electrons in the N material from moving across into the P material. But when light photons strike the junction, they give some electrons enough additional energy to overcome the opposition and cross over. Thus the current through the semiconductor will tend to increase in proportion to the brightness of the light striking it. This is the principle of the phototransistor and of other semiconductor light-sensitive devices.

The N-P-N junction transistor in a semiconductor photoelectric relay is normally in a practically nonconducting state, as is the phototransistor when in the dark. Light photons, striking the P-N junction of the phototransistor, cause it to pass current into the base of the N-P-N unit, which then also conducts strongly enough to magnetize the relay coil and close the system contacts.

In addition to an "off-on" switching operation as described, the photoelectric device can also measure light of smoothly varying intensity. The photographer's light meter makes use of a copper-oxide or similar photovoltaic cell. Here the photons give their energy to loosely-bound electrons and develop a proportional electrical voltage, just like a battery, between a copper plate and an overlying thin layer of copper oxide. This voltage, proportional to the intensity of the light, operates a sensitive milli-voltmeter calibrated in light intensity. A similar device controls the lens opening in the automatic camera. An electron photo-tube and amplifier, similar to that first described, is used by astronomers to measure the light from distant stars.

As interesting as these and many other applications of photoelectricity seem, the science of photoelectricity has revealed more of the nature of light and of matter than would have been possible with the knowledge and equipment available before.

A photovoltaic cell is a device that produces a flow of electrons when exposed to light. The silicon photovoltaic cell is produced by *doping* one section of a silicon crystal with boron to produce a P-type region. An N-type region is produced by doping with phosphorous. Contacts are attached to the photovoltaic cell and the cell is ready to produce electricity. Other materials used to make photovoltaic cells are gallium arsenide, cadmium sulfide, and cadmium telluride.

Very thin wafers of the photovoltaic material are used as cells. Many thousands of cells hooked together are capable of producing enough electric energy to power satellites.

The photovoltaic cell is the most efficient means available for converting sunlight directly into electricity, but the efficiency of the cell is too low to compete with other power sources. The efficiency of *solar cells* is increasing as new materials are used to make cells. Also, the cost of production of cells is decreasing. The combination of a decrease in cost and an increase in efficiency may eventually lead to the use of photovoltaic cells as a major source of electricity.   C.F.R./A.J.H.

SEE ALSO: AUTOMATION, ELECTRICITY, ELECTRONICS, LIGHT, PHOTOCHEMISTRY, TELEVISION, TRANSISTOR, VACUUM TUBE

Photography Photography is the process of producing images on a surface. Basic to the entire process is the chemical reaction of certain substances to light. Light rays affect things in different ways: skin turns red, colors often fade, grass and flowers grow.

About 150 years ago, chemists discovered that silver salts (combinations of silver and bromine or silver and chlorine) were affected by light. They found that if they put a coating of silver salt on a glass plate, or transparent paper, the light would affect the silver salts so that an invisible change took place where the light hit. If this paper or plate were then bathed in a special solution, the change could be made visible where the silver salt changed into silver. The untouched silver salt could then be dissolved in another solution and only the parts changed by light would remain.

One of the earlier processes, becoming popular around 1839, was introduced by a French inventor, L. J. M. Daguerre. He made use of silver plates or copper plates coated with silver, on which photographs were produced. These photographs were called *daguerreotypes,* and were sometimes called *tintypes.*

THE PHOTOGRAPHIC PROCESS

Light source: Light from the sun or a flash bulb falls on the object to be photographed. The object reflects some of the light rays and absorbs some of them. The lighter colors reflect more of the light rays.

Camera: The pattern of reflected light rays from the object is focused by the camera's lens on a film coated with silver salts. The camera must be light-tight so no other light rays can enter.

Film: A latent (invisible) image of the object is impressed upon the film by the reaction of the silver salts to the light rays.

Negative: Three solutions are needed in a darkroom. The picture, or visible image, is brought out when the film is placed in a *developer* solution; another solution stops any further development; a third solution, or *fixer,* dissolves the silver salt which has not been affected by light. In these three solutions, a "negative" picture is made. The white objects look black, the blacks are clear.

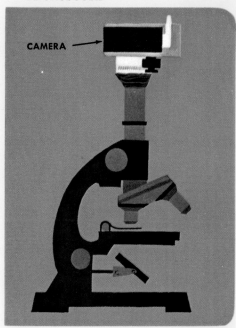

✳ **THINGS TO DO**

TAKING PICTURES THROUGH A MICROSCOPE

CAMERA →

1 **Place a microscopic slide under the objective on the stage of the microscope. Direct as much light as possible upon the specimen to be photographed.**
2 **Using electricians' tape, seal the lens opening of the camera directly over the eyepiece of the microscope.**
3 **Set the range finder on infinity. While taking the picture be careful not to jar the instruments.**
4 **Microphotography takes patience, experience, and a knowledge of general photography.**

Prints: Light must pass through the negative to shine on paper coated with silver salt in the same manner as the film. Again a latent image is formed, which is then developed and fixed. The black objects now look white, as in the original, and the clear areas, where the light penetrates and hits the paper, are dark. If the negative is placed directly against the printing paper, the process is called *contact printing.* This is used for much amateur photography. Enlargements are made by projecting the light through the negative onto the printing paper some distance away.

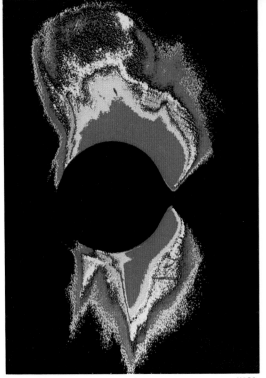

This photo of the sun's corona was taken from Skylab through a special telescope.

VARIATIONS IN THE PHOTOGRAPHIC PROCESS

Art: By special lighting, light filters, camera lenses, exposure times, developing and printing techniques, a great many different effects can be created in photography. The subject matter may be so emphasized that artistic relationships and interesting compositional arrangements are achieved.

Photoengraving: A negative is made by taking a picture of a drawing or photograph. An image is produced on a coated metal plate, which is then etched by acid, the acid affecting the parts of the plate unaffected by light in the PRINTING process. When inked and printed, the etched-away areas are the light areas.

Photomicrography involves taking pictures of the images produced by a microscope.

Astronomical photography uses lenses of large diameter and long exposure times to capture the faint light from distant stars.

Underwater photography requires special water-and-pressure-proof cameras and lighting below 20 feet (6.1 meters).

Spectrography uses infrared, ultraviolet, and X-ray films which have been sensitized to wave lengths shorter or longer than those of the visible spectrum.

High-speed photography employs a very bright flash, powered electronically, extremely short exposure times, and very sensitive "fast" film. Such rapidly moving objects as revolving wheels and the beating of insect wings can be photographed at high speed, then slowed down for viewing.

Aerial photography uses multiple lenses and high-speed shutters to take pictures of the ground for map making.

PHOTOGRAPHIC THEORY

In ordinary negative processing, the most common developers are *hydroquinone* and *monomethylparaminophenol* (trade names Elon, Metol). Developers are able to distinguish between the exposed and unexposed silver halide and convert the exposed halide to silver. Fixing solutions of *sodium* or *ammonium thiosulfate* (hypo and ammonium hypo) then dissolve out the unchanged silver halide.

It is possible to treat the film in the camera so that the final result is a positive instead of a negative. This is called *photographic reversal* and is used in some motion picture and color photography. Here the film is placed first in the developer, then in a solution of *potassium dichromate* acidified with sulfuric acid, which will dissolve the developed negative silver image, but not affect the undeveloped silver halide. After exposure to light, a positive image is produced from the remaining silver halide by developing it a second time. Thus the same film that was in the camera becomes the positive. In MOTION PICTURES, light shines through the moving positive film to reproduce the original scene—enlarged—on a screen.

Color photography involves the use of a special film containing three separate layers which record the red, blue, and green wave lengths of the visible spectrum. Because all colors can be made of mixtures of red, blue, and green, they are called *primary* colors.

Color film can be developed by the reversal process, producing positive transparencies viewed by projection. Another kind of color film is developed so that the negative shows the opposite color values; red looks blue-green, blue looks yellow, green looks magenta. Printing reproduces the original colors. H.W.M.

SEE ALSO: LENS, MAN-MADE; OCEANOGRAPHY; PHOTOCHEMISTRY; PHOTOMETER; SPECTROSCOPE; TELESCOPE; X-RAY.

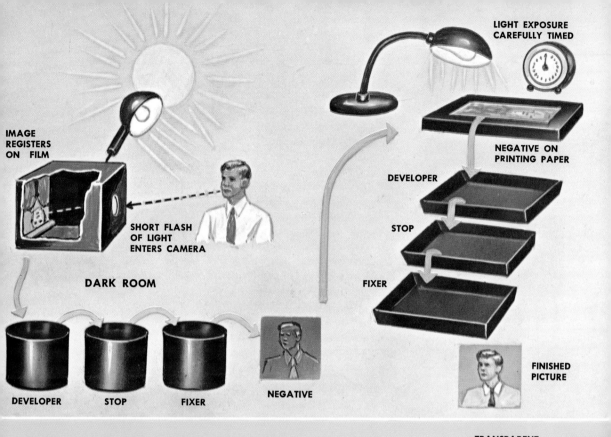

IMAGE REGISTERS ON FILM

SHORT FLASH OF LIGHT ENTERS CAMERA

DARK ROOM

DEVELOPER

STOP

FIXER

NEGATIVE

LIGHT EXPOSURE CAREFULLY TIMED

NEGATIVE ON PRINTING PAPER

DEVELOPER

STOP

FIXER

FINISHED PICTURE

For still camera
A. Improper setting for high speed

B. Proper setting for high speed

For motion picture. In viewing, A can be slowed down to appear as B.

TRANSPARENT COLOR SLIDE

RED

PRIMARY COLORS PRODUCE COLOR IMAGE

BLUE

YELLOW

X-RAY PHOTOGRAPH OF A JEEP

Marvin English

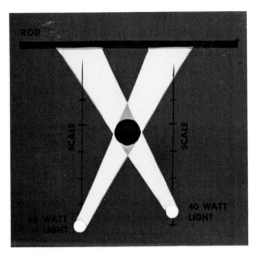

The shadow photometer requires the movement of light source until shadows are equally illuminated to compare their illuminating power

Photometer (foh-TOHM-eh-ter) The photometer is an OPTICAL INSTRUMENT used for measuring the intensity of a light source, such as a light bulb. The eye is not capable of directly comparing two light sources, but it can compare the brightness of two similar surfaces. If the color of the two surfaces is the same, the eye can detect quite small differences in brightness.

Photoelectric devices measure the intensity of light. They are capable of accurate comparisons of light sources. Once calibrated, photoelectric photometers can determine the intensity of an unknown source.

Difficulty arises if the eye tries to make a comparison between two sources of different color. Lamps of different color may be compared by using a flicker photometer. This device enables the observer to view one side of the screen and then the other in relatively rapid succession. A frequency will be found where the flicker due to color difference will disappear, and the colors seemingly blend into a single hue. The flicker due to illumination will still appear, however. If the screen is moved, a position can be found where this flicker will also disappear. The illumination can be calculated, using an equation. A rotating prism is used to view both sides of the screen alternately.   A.E.L.

SEE ALSO: COLOR, LIGHT

Photon (FOH-tahn) A photon is the elementary bundle or packet of electromagnetic energy absorbed or emitted by an atom or a molecule. Electromagnetic energy travels as a set of waves. But the emission or absorption of the electromagnetic energy occurs only in units called *quanta*. A quantum of energy is the energy carried by a single photon.

When an atom loses energy by passing from one state to another, it must satisfy the principle of conservation of energy. The energy lost is taken up by some other atom or given off in some form of radiation.

Niels Bohr, a Danish physicist, adopted the *energy packet* idea from Max Planck, a professor at the University of Berlin. There were certain phenomena, such as the photoelectric effect, which indicated that light did not always behave as a wave. The packet theory states that energy can be emitted or absorbed only in small but definite amounts, called quanta or photons.   A. E. L.
SEE ALSO: PHOTOELECTRICITY, QUANTUM THEORY

Photosphere (FOH-tuh-sfihr) The great, visible, yellow face of the sun is called the photosphere. Photosphere means "light sphere." The photosphere is about 864,000 miles (1,390,000 kilometers) in diameter. Above it are the *chromosphere* and the *corona*, both gaseous in nature. They extend for thousands of miles or kilometers above the photosphere.

The sun's photosphere is not uniform in its brightness. A specially equipped telescope will reveal that there are patches of darkness. These are *sunspots.* They appear to be areas of calm in an otherwise violent atmosphere. Large sunspots may be close to 100,000 miles (161,000 kilometers) in diameter. The appearance and surface of the photosphere are constantly changing because the number and location of sunspots change from time to time in a regular cycle.   H.S.G.

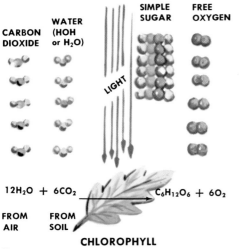

SIMPLE SUGAR

FREE OXYGEN

CARBON DIOXIDE

WATER (HOH or H₂O)

LIGHT

$12H_2O + 6CO_2 \longrightarrow C_6H_{12}O_6 + 6O_2$

FROM AIR   **FROM SOIL**

CHLOROPHYLL

© **CARBON**

© **OXYGEN**

© **HYDROGEN**

Photosynthesis (foh-toe-SIN-thuh-sis) A plant is like a little factory. It will take several things, put them together with the help of light, and end up with something new. Making food by plants is called photosynthesis. This word can be broken into two words: *photo* meaning "light" and *synthesis* meaning "put together." Only green plants can take water from the soil, carbon dioxide from the air, and with the help of light, make sugar. Since plants do not use all of the oxygen for food-making, it is given off. Animals need plants for food and oxygen.

Photosynthesis is a chemical change which occurs in all green cells. Only green plants are able to take the sun's energy and put it into a stored form for use by other plants and animals. Scientists know most of the materials and steps involved in this wonderful process yet are still unable to accomplish this in the laboratory. There is a secret about green plant cells that man has not discovered as yet. The equation for photosynthesis is as follows:

$$12H_2O + 6CO_2 + \text{light}$$
$$\rightarrow C_6H_{12}O_6 + 6O_2 + 6H_2O$$

water + $\begin{matrix}\text{carbon}\\\text{dioxide}\end{matrix}$ → sugar + oxygen + water

The electromagnetic energy contained in sunlight is converted by photosynthesis to chemical energy stored in the sugar mole-

✳ **THINGS TO DO**

DO LEAVES MAKE FOOD?

1 Remove a leaf from a plant that has been in the sunlight for several hours.
2 Partly submerge a small container of alcohol into boiling water. Alcohol should not be heated directly over a flame. When the alcohol is boiling put the leaf into it.
3 The chlorophyll will be removed. When the leaf is white spread it on the surface of a dish.
4 Put several drops of iodine on the leaf. If starch (food) is present, it will become a deep blue.

cule. The sugar can then be converted into starch and stored.

The rate of photosynthesis is dependent upon several conditions. A greater amount of available water will increase the rate of photosynthesis. Food-making occurs best in a temperature range from 68° to 110° F. (20° to 43.3° C.). The amount of carbon dioxide in the air is important. The air contains ½ per cent of carbon dioxide and a plant can use up to 5 per cent concentration; therefore this is a limiting factor. The amount and nature of the light controls photosynthesis. Food production is most active in about ⅒ of full sunlight. Too much light tends to destroy some of the products of photosynthesis.

Food manufactured in the leaves or other green parts of a plant is transported to various parts and stored for future use. Most annual plants store food in their seeds. Biennials and perennials also store food in their roots, stems, and leaves. H.J.C.

SEE ALSO: BALANCE OF NATURE, CARBON CYCLE, LEAVES, PLANT

Phototropism see Tropism

The shape and size of a solid is limited by its locked molecules

Phylogeny (fih-LOJ-eh-neye) Phylogeny is the study of ancestral relationships. Different kinds of animals are found to be related because they have similar body plans, development, larvae, or structures of like origin.

SEE ALSO: ANIMALS, CLASSIFICATION OF; EVOLUTION OF MAN; PLANTS, CLASSIFICATION OF

The shape of liquid can be spherical if outside forces do not interfere, otherwise it will take the form of the container it occupies

Physical states and changes Physical states and changes involve the study of matter. All MATTER takes up space and has weight. All matter has three physical states: solid, liquid and gas. Heat, or the lack of heat, changes matter from one state to another. Water can exist in three different states. Water in the form of ice in a refrigerator is in its solid physical state. Water coming from a faucet is in its liquid physical state. Water boiling in a tea pot turns to steam, its gaseous physical state. Through all these physical changes, the substance itself—water remains the same.

Matter can neither be created nor destroyed by ordinary means. The physical states of matter can be changed or matter can be combined with other forms of matter to make new substances.

All matter, solid, liquid or gas, is alike in two ways. A block of wood, a glass of water, or air, all occupy space. Air, and other gases, may appear not to take up space. However, if a drinking glass is turned over and pressed down in a bowl of water, water will enter the glass only part way because the air in the glass does occupy space. The space occupied by a material is called its *volume*. All material has weight. Solids, such as a brick, or liquids, such as water in a bucket, obviously have weight. That air has weight is shown by the difference in weights of a deflated and an inflated basketball.

Solids have the characteristics of keeping a definite shape and having a definite volume. A pencil or a brick does not change shape by itself, nor does it change the amount of space it occupies.

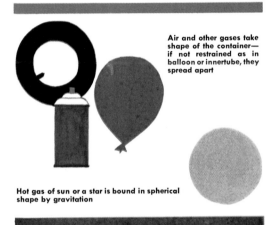

Air and other gases take shape of the container—if not restrained as in balloon or innertube, they spread apart

Hot gas of sun or a star is bound in spherical shape by gravitation

Liquids, like solids, take up a given amount of volume. A glass of milk occupies a certain amount of space, but if the milk is poured into a pan, it takes the shape of the pan. A liquid, not having a shape of its own, takes the shape of the container it fills. Therefore, a liquid has volume, but no constant shape.

Gas has no form of its own. Air in a covered drinking glass takes the shape of the glass. A gas does not occupy a definite amount of space. Air in a bottle, if uncorked, spreads into the room. A gas, then, is matter in a state in which it has no definite shape nor volume. Gases will expand to fill any container.

Very often matter in one state is combined with matter in another state. Mixing sugar into lemonade combines a liquid material with a solid material. In a solution these things happen. First, the liquid in a solution is clear and free of particles. Secondly, the dissolved material can pass through the finest of filters which allows the liquid to pass. The dissolved material cannot be filtered out. Thirdly, the dissolved material spreads evenly throughout the solution medium.

Special apparatus, such as a molecular still (left), perform operations in molecular research. Substances to be irradiated are placed inside a nuclear radiation chamber (right) with a highly radioactive sample. The chamber is an aid to physicists in their study of radiation

Some solid materials added to a liquid do not go into solution, but are suspended in the liquid. Starch and water when combined do not form a solution. Rather, a suspension of the starch particles occurs.

Changes from one physical state to another can occur by heating or by taking away heat. When a solid is heated enough, it changes to a liquid. For example, a piece of aluminum melts when heated to 1220° F. (660° C.). Liquids, when heated enough, change to gases. Water changes to steam at 212° F. (100° C.). Liquids may also evaporate at low temperatures. For example, water evaporates from wet clothes hanging on a line.

Cooling the materials of each state of matter reverses the physical changes. Gas will turn to a liquid, and liquid, when cooled enough, will become a solid.   P.F.D.

SEE ALSO: ATOM, CHEMICAL CHANGE, CHEMISTRY, EVAPORATION, GAS, HEAT, LIQUID, MOLECULAR THEORY, PHYSICS, SOLID, SOLUBLE, SOLUTION

Physics (FIZZ-icks) Physics is the science that deals mainly with the fundamental qualities of energy and non-living matter. Energy is the ability or capacity to do work; matter is anything that has MASS and occupies space. There are many forms of energy such as mechanical energy, light, sound, magnetic energy, electrical energy, and heat.

MATHEMATICS is an important tool in the study of physics. The science is concerned with the natural laws which govern the environment of man and theories about the behavior of matter. The pull of GRAVITY which causes weight is an illustration of the Universal Law of Gravitation, an important law in physics. Theories may change when experiments give new evidence about the nature of matter. The atomic theory illustrates how a theory may be modified. At first, atoms of matter were thought to contain only a few particles. Now the atomic theory must account for over twenty different particles which have been discovered.

Physics is an exact science. A knowledge of physics is obtained by application of scientific methods: getting data, forming hypotheses, and testing the hypotheses by applied experiments. The division of physics into areas of study according to form of energy may include: mechanics, heat, sound, light, magnetism, electricity, atomic, and nuclear. Physics can also be divided by fields of specialization: statics, dynamics, wave mechanics, cryogenics, classical physics, electronics, quantum mechanics, relativity, and high-energy physics. Physics is also combined with

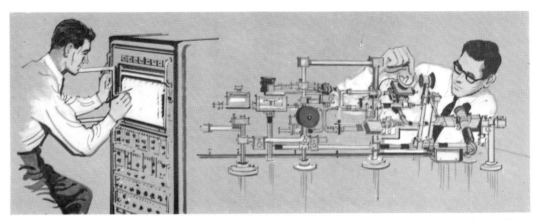

Recording and measuring instruments are designed to study substances under varied conditions. Specialized instruments and equipment enable the physicist to determine the nature of matter

other fields of science such as astrophysics, biophysics, physical chemistry, geophysics, and space physics.

Mechanics involves a broad area of knowledge, especially the topics of motion, force, energy, solids, liquids, and gases. Mechanics includes a study of many fundamental quantities and their measurement. These include the concepts of mass, weight, density, and volume. Some of these are VECTOR quantities that have not only numerical value but a definite direction. Weight, the pull of gravity on an object, is directed toward the earth and illustrates a vector quantity. Mass refers to the amount of matter in an object and is not a vector, or directional, quantity. Mass would not change even if gravity changed. Studies of *potential* and *kinetic* energy are part of mechanics. Potential energy is stored up energy such as water in a dam. This energy becomes kinetic when the water flows over the dam to run a HYDROELECTRIC POWER plant.

HEAT, another form of energy, is studied for its nature and behavior. The quantity of heat a body contains is measured in calories or British Thermal Units. Temperature indicates the intensity of heat but not its quantity. In terms of the MOLECULAR THEORY of heat, temperature is the average kinetic energy of the molecules of matter, but the quantity of heat is the total kinetic energy. Studies of RADIATION, conduction, and convection are included as methods of heat transfer.

The physics of SOUND concerns how sounds are produced and transmitted. Energy is required to make objects vibrate and send out sound waves. Sound waves are longitudinal, and in air, air particles vibrate back and forth in the same direction as the sound wave travels. The study of sound includes the special properties of musical sounds—pitch, loudness, and quality.

LIGHT as a form of energy requires two theories to fully explain its behavior. The *wave theory* of light holds for light as a transverse wave motion, an electromagnetic wave, which travels with a velocity of 186,000 miles (300,000 kilometers) per second. The *quantum theory* explains how atoms absorb and emit light energy. The energy is given off or taken up in small bundles rather than in a continuous manner.

ELECTRICITY is another broad area of physics. It includes a study of electric charges, magnetism, and current electricity. Electricity is used in many electrical devices such as motors, generators, batteries, transformers, and electronic equipment.

Rapid advances in physics in recent decades have occurred in atomic and nuclear physics. This area includes electrical discharge in gases, electromagnetic and spectral series, and X-rays. Research in NUCLEAR ENERGY, radioactivity, and atomic disintegration has brought dramatic results. The atomic bomb demonstrated how tremendous amounts of energy may be released when a small amount of matter is converted into energy.

There are also specialized areas in physics dealing with physical properties of living matter. BIOPHYSICS is the study of living things using the methods and tools of physics. The theories and facts of physics are so basic they are involved in almost every other science.   L. M.

WILLIAM
HARVEY

ISAAC
NEWTON

BENJAMIN
FRANKLIN

ANTOINE
LAVOISIER

Physiology Physiology is the study of how living structures work. For example, in order to keep alive, all living things get ENERGY from food. They grow and reproduce new living forms just like themselves. They react to the world around them, and try to adjust to changes. As plant and animal life becomes larger and more complicated, the different parts of a body must be coordinated so they work together. Physiology studies these processes.

Because the scientist must first understand how a thing is made before he can understand how it works, a physiologist studies the various parts of the living structure—its ANATOMY. He studies the functioning of the structure. He may study how an individual NERVE CELL sends an impulse, how the muscles of the body move together, or why a plant produces flowers at certain times of the year. But to have an understanding of the building materials of living things and the natural laws governing them, a physiologist must also know the basic PHYSICS and CHEMISTRY of the nonliving world, as well as the biophysics and biochemistry of living structures.

For example a boy or girl eats food and grows bigger. The physiologist checks digestion, circulation, elimination, metabolism, respiration, and excretion to find out what is happening to the food inside the person's body.

DIGESTION

When food enters the mouth, it is chewed by the teeth into small pieces, mixed with saliva produced by the salivary glands, and passed down the esophagus into the stomach. Once in the stomach, an acid mixture of enzymes begins the digestion of the food

IMPORTANT DISCOVERIES IN PHYSIOLOGY AND RELATED FIELDS

1600 Fabricius studies human anatomy and writes book <u>About Venous Valves</u>.

1628 Harvey publishes <u>Motion of the Heart and Blood</u>.

1650 Boyle invents air pumps and studies lung-pressure.

1656 Wharton is first to study gland physiology.

1661 Malpighi describes mechanism of breathing; later studies kidney secretion.

1670 Borelli studies the physics of animal movement.

1687 Newton publishes his <u>Principles</u> that lay the foundation for all exact sciences.

1688 Leeuwenhoek discovers capillaries with his microscope.

1733 Hales writes about blood pressure.

1752 Franklin shows that lightning is electricity; shows some electrostatic actions on the body.

1774 Priestly discovers oxygen.

1777 Spallanzani studies how foods digest—in test tubes.

1780 Lavoisier refines Priestley's ideas about air and oxygen; and shows similarity of burning and breathing.

1791 Galvani discovers the effects of electricity on muscles.

1796 Jenner successfully uses first vaccine and immunizes people against smallpox.

1821 Magendie experiments on nerves acting on muscles and glands.

1839 Schleiden and Schwann offer evidence that cells are basic life units.

1846 Long and Morton use first safe anesthetic, ether.

by chemical action, and the mechanical churning of the muscular stomach wall aids in this digestion. When the food has been broken down into a thick, soupy liquid, it passes through an opening into the small intestine a little at a time. In the small intestine the most important part of digestion begins. First, the acid solution is made slightly alkaline. Separate ENZYMES, which are specific in their action, are secreted by the cells of the intestinal wall and pancreas. These enzymes break down starches into sugar, fats into glycerol and fatty acids, proteins into amino acids. The liver forms a substance to break fat into small droplets. Secretions from pancreas and liver reach the small intestine through ducts. The coordination of all this enzyme activity is controlled by hormones circulating in the blood.

CIRCULATION

When all the large molecules of food have been reduced to small molecules by digestion, the particular substances that the body needs to build new tissue are available. First, however, these small molecules must be taken inside the cells throughout all parts of the body, for it is within each small cell that new tissue is made. From the digestive tract the blood receives the small molecules that can be used as building blocks for new tissue, and transports them through the body. They travel through the network of blood and lymph vessels, and are propelled by the pumping action of the heart.

ELIMINATION

The part of the food that cannot be used by the body passes from the small intestine into the large intestine and rectum. It is discarded as feces after such important substances as water and vitamin K have been restored to the body.

METABOLISM

Once the small molecular building blocks are brought within the cells of the body, the formation of new tissue begins. Hormones circulating through the blood regulate the amount and kind of tissue formation and the places in the body where new tissue will be formed. The chromatin material in the nucleus of each cell provides the pattern of tissue formation and the enzymes that make it possible.

When a person is little, the growth hormone of the PITUITARY gland stimulates a high rate of protein synthesis and, conse-

quently, rapid growth. As he reaches PUBERTY, the long bones of the body and the masses of muscle tissue are conspicuous areas of growth. When he becomes an adult, the amount of new tissue formed is normally only enough to keep pace with the damage produced during the wear and tear of living.

RESPIRATION

In order to make new tissue, there must be energy provided by the body to link together the small building blocks into those particular large molecules needed by the body. There are definite chemical reactions that take place in the cell and provide this energy. These reactions require oxygen, which is obtained from the air by respiration. To bring oxygen to the cell, the boy's lungs, aided by the muscular action of the diaphragm and the chest muscles, breathe in air. Once again, it is the pumping action of the heart that drives the oxygen-bearing blood through the body to reach each individual cell. The respiratory muscles are controlled by the brain, and function automatically without the boy's being consciously aware of doing this work. Indeed, many parts of the body function automatically in this way, and free large areas of the brain for observing and evaluating the outside world.

EXCRETION

The creation of energy and the synthesis of new tissue results in wastes that must be removed from the body. If these wastes remain in the body, they poison it. The liver detoxicates nitrogenous wastes, and these products are then carried by the blood stream to the kidney for removal as urine. The water balance of the body is a crucial physiological necessity, and this balance is maintained by the functioning of the kidney and supervised by endocrine hormones.

ADAPTATION

The delicate physiological balance (*homeostasis*) needed by the body for it to function properly is a never-ending study. As the biochemical reactions proceed within the body—the processes of digestion, respiration, muscular activity, or secretion of hormones—new products accumulate, and old reserves of raw material are used up. There are continuous changes going on inside the body, and adjustments must be made continuously to preserve the conditions necessary for life. These adaptations are, for the most part, set into motion by the nervous system and the endocrine secretions.

Outside the body, changes are also influencing the physiology. If the aroma of food reaches the hungry boy's nostrils, he gets ready to eat. If he is riding his bicycle and loses his balance around a curve in the road, the nervous system and muscles cooperate to keep him from falling and injuring himself. If it suddenly becomes cold, the nervous system alerts the boy to put on warmer clothing. If infectious germs enter the body, the defenses of inflammation, reaction, and *phagocytosis* go to work.

These physiological processes proceed in every living organism, whether it is a one-celled body or a complex many-celled body. The simpler the organism, of course, the less elaborate the mechanisms necessary to sustain life.

For example, a one-celled alga plant is able to take in food and release wastes by means of its semipermeable cell membrane. Simple diffusion circulates the particles within the cell. In the earthworm there are many cells, and although the animal is relatively small in size, it still requires a special network of tissues to distribute nourishment and remove wastes. The human body has evolved complex organ systems to insure nutrition, waste removal, and physiological harmony.

Indeed, all the systems involved in physiology are so complex that research proceeds continually to discover the secrets of life that still elude man's understanding.   B. B. G.
SEE ALSO: ADAPTATION, CIRCULATORY SYSTEM, DIGESTIVE SYSTEM, ENDOCRINE GLANDS, EXCRETORY SYSTEM, HISTOLOGY, HOMEOSTASIS, METABOLISM, MUSCLE SYSTEM, NERVOUS SYSTEM, NUTRITION, REPRODUCTIVE SYSTEMS, RESPIRATORY SYSTEM, SENSE ORGANS, STRESS

Physiotherapy

Physiotherapy Physiotherapy is the treatment of weakened body muscles by physical means such as massage, heat, and exercise.

Physical therapy and its offshoot, occupational therapy, play an important part in any hospital. Patients who have had strokes or brain or spinal cord injuries must learn to walk and talk again. Those who have had amputations or have been in bed a long time

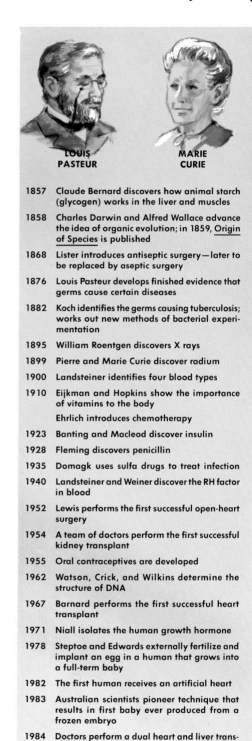

LOUIS PASTEUR   MARIE CURIE

1857 Claude Bernard discovers how animal starch (glycogen) works in the liver and muscles

1858 Charles Darwin and Alfred Wallace advance the idea of organic evolution; in 1859, Origin of Species is published

1868 Lister introduces antiseptic surgery—later to be replaced by aseptic surgery

1876 Louis Pasteur develops finished evidence that germs cause certain diseases

1882 Koch identifies the germs causing tuberculosis; works out new methods of bacterial experimentation

1895 William Roentgen discovers X rays

1899 Pierre and Marie Curie discover radium

1900 Landsteiner identifies four blood types

1910 Eijkman and Hopkins show the importance of vitamins to the body

       Ehrlich introduces chemotherapy

1923 Banting and Macleod discover insulin

1928 Fleming discovers penicillin

1935 Domagk uses sulfa drugs to treat infection

1940 Landsteiner and Weiner discover the RH factor in blood

1952 Lewis performs the first successful open-heart surgery

1954 A team of doctors perform the first successful kidney transplant

1955 Oral contraceptives are developed

1962 Watson, Crick, and Wilkins determine the structure of DNA

1967 Barnard performs the first successful heart transplant

1971 Niall isolates the human growth hormone

1978 Steptoe and Edwards externally fertilize and implant an egg in a human that grows into a full-term baby

1982 The first human receives an artificial heart

1983 Australian scientists pioneer technique that results in first baby ever produced from a frozen embryo

1984 Doctors perform a dual heart and liver transplant on a six-year-old girl who is first to recover from a dual transplant

1985 Harvard Medical School scientists make the first discovery of a human protein, angiogenin, that stimulates growth of blood vessels which may aid in cancer treatment

1991 Researchers synthesize polio virus in a lab, the first time a virus is created outside living cells

can learn to use artifical limbs or strengthen weakened muscles.

Physical therapy can include whirlpool baths, heat treatments, exercise machines, and walkers and canes. In addition, people who are confined to bed can learn to busy themselves with the help of occupational therapists who can teach skills such as needlepoint, weaving, and rug hooking.   E.S.S.

Piccard, Auguste (1884-1962) Auguste Piccard was the twin brother of Jean Piccard. He was a Swiss physicist who foresaw SPACE TRAVEL by means of rockets. In 1932 he prepared the way for interplanetary travel by ascending 53,152 feet (16,200 meters) into the stratosphere in an airtight gondola suspended beneath a BALLOON.

In 1953 he broke another record, this time by descending 10,330 feet (3,149 meters) under the sea in a steel sphere attached to tanks filled with gasoline. These tanks were pulled down into the water by weights controlled by electromagnetic current. When the current was turned off, the tanks brought the sphere to the surface of the water.

Piccard was born in Basle, Switzerland, in 1884. He was graduated as a mechanical engineer from the University of Basle and the Institute of Technology at Zürich.   D.H.J.
SEE ALSO: BATHYSPHERE AND BATHYSCAPHE, OCEANOGRAPHY

Piccard, Jacques see Bathysphere and bathyscaphe

Piccard, Jean (1884-1963) Jean Piccard was a Swiss physicist who, in 1934, ascended 57,549 feet (17,540 meters) into the stratosphere at Dearborn, Michigan. Three years later he tested the possibility of using a number of large balloons to carry an open gondola into the atmosphere. The one hundred balloons he used were 6 feet (1.8 meters) in diameter.

Unlike his brother Auguste, Jean came to the United States in 1916 where he taught at the University of Chicago for three years. Returning to his native Switzerland, he taught at the University of Lausanne until 1926 when he returned to the United States to accept a post as instructor at the Massachusetts Institute of Technology. In 1931 he became a citizen of the United States, and five years later he joined the faculty of the University of Minnesota. Jean Piccard was born and educated in Switzerland.   D.H.J.

Pickerel see Pike

Pickle see Cucumber

Pickling Pickling (in metallurgy) is the removal, by the use of acids, of the scale, or OXIDE layer, which forms when metals are heated for rolling or forging. Pickling (in food processing) is preservation with BRINE.
SEE: METAL

Picric acid see Carbolic acid

Piezoelectric effect When crystals of certain materials are subjected to a mechanical STRESS, they generate electromotive force. If these crystals are subjected to an alternating electrical stress, they vibrate. The relationship between the mechanical and electrical properties of the CRYSTAL is the piezoelectric effect.

Quartz, rochelle salts, and tourmaline all exhibit the piezoelectric effect. Quartz crystals are used to control the frequency output of transmitters or any other equipment where exact frequency control is required. Rochelle salts are used in microphones; tourmaline may be used in pressure gauges.
D. A. B.

SEE ALSO: PHOTOELECTRICITY

The stress produced by a hammer hitting a crystal may produce enough electricity to light a small bulb

Common pigeon, or rock dove

James P. Rowan
Pigs have been domesticated for centuries.

Pig The pig family includes both wild and domestic hogs. The word *pig* is usually used to refer to a baby hog. The mother hog is called a *sow* and the father, a *boar*. Hogs are also called *swine*. Farmers raise large quantities of hogs mainly for their tasty meat.

Pigs have a round, heavy body, short legs, and a short tail. Their feet have an even number of hoofed toes. Short bristles grow from their thick skin. Their tough snouts are used for lifting, pushing and digging. Wild pigs are especially strong and fierce. Pigs, or their relative, the PECCARY, are found in almost all temperate areas except Australia. Pigs will eat almost anything.

Hogs were tamed by man as early as the STONE AGE. They may be found on farms in all parts of the world. Man has learned to use almost every part of the hog's body. He eats its flesh (bacon, ham, pork, sausage, spareribs) as well as its stomach, kidneys, liver, ears, brain, skin, snout and jowls. Its fat is rendered (extracting by melting) for lard, skin is tanned for leather, and bristles are used for brushes.

There are many different breeds of hogs. Selective breeding has developed one that produces a maximum of lean meat and a minimum of fat (lard).

Pigs are good breeders. A sow may have two or three litters a year. Each litter may include eight to 25 or more little pigs. A sow may have as many as 28 nipples, more than any other animal. A piglet grows to marketable size, about 200 pounds (91 kilograms), in about six months.   D.J.A.
SEE ALSO: ARTIODACTYLA, HOOF

Pig iron see Iron

Pigeon There are about 120 species of birds in the pigeon family. Two types are found throughout North America. They can be distinguished by the shape of the tail. Common domestic pigeons have fan-shaped tails. Other pigeons, such as the mourning dove, have pointed or short, rounded tails. There is actually very little difference between doves and pigeons. Usually the smaller birds in the family are called doves and the larger ones pigeons. Pigeons vary in color, and their coloring is often iridescent. These birds are all related to the European rock dove.

Pigeons are broad breasted with small, rounded heads. They are seed eaters, but they usually swallow seeds instead of crushing them. Thus jaw muscles for closing are not well developed. *Nares* or nostrils are covered by a fleshy flap or *operculum*. Many pigeons lack oil glands for preening feathers. They are one of the few birds to drink water without lifting their heads.

Pigeons' flight averages 60 miles (96.5 kilometers) per hour. They have well-developed *pectoral* (breast) muscles and a deep keel on the *sternum* (breastbone) to which the wings are attached.

Almost all pigeons lay two white eggs. Tropical species, however, lay fewer eggs than northern ones. Both sexes incubate the eggs. Young are naked at birth and are cared for in the carelessly made nest. They are fed "pigeon milk," a diet made up of partially disintegrated cells from the lining of the parent's enlarged gullet (*crop*).

Mature pigeons feed on small nuts, seeds, and grain. They can easily be trained to come for such foods as popcorn or peanuts. J. C. K.
SEE ALSO: FOWL

WHAT HAPPENS WHEN TWO OR MORE PIGMENTS ARE MIXED TOGETHER?

1   Water colors or oil paints may be used for this experiment. The object is to mix two different colors to determine the color of the resulting mixture.
2   Mix a small amount of yellow pigment to the same amount of blue pigment. What color is it now?
3   Try a combination of red and blue pigments, then red and yellow. Save each mixture.
4   Blend a small quantity of two of these together to obtain still another color. Record the results each time and draw conclusions.
5   Does there seem to be a pattern to pigment combinations? You will find that, unlike combining colored lights, pigment colors are subtracted by others. The color that is left is the one that is transmitted to your eyes.

Pigment Pigment is the substance which gives color to paint, to leaves, to skin, and to hair. Mineral pigment is used as a fine powder and can be mixed with liquids to form PAINT (the pigment does not dissolve in the liquid). Shellacs and varnishes show the surface beneath them because they do not contain pigment. Two common paint pigments are *iron oxide* and *zinc oxide*.

The pigment in the deeper epidermal layers of the SKIN that makes the difference in color in various races is called *melanin*. It is also the pigment of suntan.

Pigments gain their colors only by reflecting parts of the light shining on them. Transparent colors, however, gain their color by allowing the passage of only certain wavelengths of LIGHT.   E.M.N.

SEE ALSO: ALBINO, COLOR

Pika see Rabbit

Pike The pike family includes the *pickerel* and *muskellunge*. These blue or greenish-gray fish are long and heavy. The heaviest is the "muskie," which weighs from 70 to 102 pounds (32 to 46 kilograms). Pikes can be told apart by the pattern of scales on their cheeks and gill covers.

Pike are meat eaters, feeding mostly on smaller fish. They have spadelike bills and very sharp teeth that show when the mouth is closed. All have swim bladders that open into the digestive tracts, fins without spines, and low-lying pectoral or ventral fins. Spawning occurs in the spring in shallow, weedy water. Two species of pike, the pickerel and muskie, are known to interbreed.

Whenever these species are present, they are the top CARNIVORES (meat eaters) in the aquatic *food chain*. They are very sensitive to slight changes in the environment, sometimes disappearing from areas where they were once very common.   J. C. K.

SEE ALSO: ECOLOGY, PISCES

Pile, atomic see Accelerators, Nuclear reactors, Nuclear science

Pilot see Aviation

Northern pike

Some pines important for lumber: western white pine (left), lodgepole pine (center) and ponderosa pine (right)

Pilot fish Pilot fish follow ships and sharks in tropical and subtropical seas. These narrow, bluish fish, with dark-blue or purple bands across their backs, grow to about 12 inches (30.5 centimeters).

Pilot fish

Pimple A pimple is a defect on the surface of the skin and usually is raised, round, and red, with or without a white center.

The word *pimple* is often used in connection with ACNE, in which there is a series of inflammations around the *sebaceous* glands of the skin, usually on the face and back. However, pimples can also result from bacteria invading the skin follicles, in which case the central white spot can be sebaceous gland sebum (a normal secretion) or yellow pus.

When the infection is most prominent, the pimple becomes a *pustule,* and when a group of pustules merge they form a *boil.* A boil in which the pus collects completely below the skin is a *wen.*   E.S.S.

Pine Pine is the common name for a large family of evergreen trees. They range in size from dwarfs to over 100 feet (30.5 meters) tall. Branches usually grow in whorls around the trunk. Pine LEAVES grow in the form of slender needles, always in groups from two to five.

Pine trees normally have a taproot, but PRUNING forces them to develop a fibrous ROOT system. They do not produce flowers. Instead, the seed-producing structure is a cone *(strobile).* Naked seeds (not enclosed in a fruit) are attached to scales of the cone.

Pine trees are very useful to man. They produce lumber, tar, pitch, oil,

The winged seeds of the white pine cone are scattered by the wind

Courtesy Society For Visual Education, Inc.

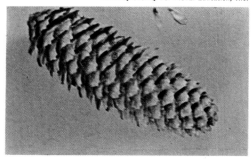

and turpentine. Seeds of some kinds are eaten by man and animals.

These plants reproduce by ALTERNATION OF GENERATIONS. The tree is a sporophyte that produces two kinds of cones and spores. Young female cones *(ovulate)* are large and borne near the top of the tree. Male cones *(staminate)* are very small, often less than one-half inch (1.3 centimeters) in length. Often noticeable only during pollinating, they usually grow on branches below the female cones. This arrangement of cones almost ensures cross-pollination, since wind rarely blows straight up.

The second generation of reproduction is caused by the union (FERTILIZATION) of pollen grains and the egg nucleus. This union begins the development of winged seeds. The whole cycle of pollination, fertilization, and seed development takes two years. Cones at maturity become brown, and the scales separate, allowing the seeds to escape. They are dispersed by wind currents. The embryo has plenty of reserve food. The embryo's strong, tough seed coat permits it to remain dormant for long periods of time.

White pine has blue-gray needles in clusters of five. Cones are slender, tapering, and thornless. This tree averages 100 feet (30.5 meters) in height. *Red* pine has dark green needles in clusters of two. Its cones are thornless. The average height of this pine is 70 feet (21.3 meters).

Needles of the *longleaf* pine measure 18 inches (45.7 centimeters) and are in groups of three. Cones have short thorns. This tree averages 60 feet (18.3 meters). *Shortleaf* pine reaches 100 feet (30.5) meters. Needles appear in clusters of two or three. This tree produces short, thorny cones.

Jack pines and *scrub* pines are smaller trees, often only 25 feet (7.6 meters) tall. The latter has 3-inch (7.6-centimeter) needles and thorny cones, while jack pine has 1½-inch (3.8-centimeter) needles and thornless cones.

Pitch pines bear stiff, twisted needles up to 5 inches (12.7 centimeters) long in clusters of three. Their broad cones have thorns.

Enemies of the pines include fungus diseases, snout beetle, bark aphid, webworms, and leaf scale. Pines are in the family Pinaceae and the class GYMNOSPERMAE. H.J.C.
SEE ALSO: FOREST PRODUCTS, LUMBER

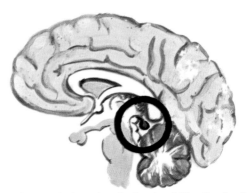

Location of the pineal gland within the brain

Pineal gland The pineal gland is located in the lower central part of the BRAIN. It may be all that remains of a third eye that ancestors of VERTEBRATES (animals with backbones) once had. An ancient-type lizard in New Zealand (SPHENODON) has a light-sensitive place on its head above the pineal body. Scientists now know that the pineal is a light-sensitive gland that makes a hormone.

The pineal gland is rich in *serotonin,* a substance secreted by the nervous system. Recently a new hormone, *melatonin,* and an enzyme found only in the pineal were isolated. Research showed that the enzyme acted on serotonin to form melatonin. Melatonin acts on the sex glands to inhibit (stop) the sexual cycle.

Light controls the amount of hormone produced through the sympathetic nervous system. The concentration of melatonin shows a 24-hour rhythm, decreasing during the day and increasing at night. J. C. K.
SEE ALSO: NERVOUS SYSTEM

Pineapple The fruit of the pineapple looks like a giant pine cone. It is a native to northern South America. It still grows wild in Brazil. Hawaii leads in the production of this fruit. The fruit may weigh 1 to 18 pounds (.5 to 8.2 kilograms). Its tough fruit wall is such protection that it can be shipped to many countries without damage.

Pineapple plant and fruit

The pineapple is a tropical BIENNIAL in the monocotyledon group of flowering plants. The leaves, having sharp points on the sides, form a rosette around a 3-foot (.9 meter) stem. The bloom is a bunch of small tightly packed flowers. The fruit that develops from this flower head is classified as *multiple,* having many ovaries and receptacles fused together. Since the fruit is usually seedless the plant must be propagated by other means: by planting slips, suckers, or the top cluster of leaves.

Besides using this plant's fruit, man also makes textile products from piña cloth woven from the white, strong fibers found in the leaves.

Pineapple also refers to a plant family (Bromeliaceae) that includes SPANISH MOSS.

H.J.C.

Pinkeye see Conjunctivitis

Pinks Pinks is a common name for a whole group of flowering plants. The group includes carnation, baby's breath, bouncing bet, campion, catchfly, and sweet William. They are HERBS which grow for one year (ANNUAL) or for more than two years (PERENNIAL). Most pinks are found in the northern regions of the United States.

LEAVES are simple with smooth margins. They are arranged opposite to each other on the stem. The stem has swollen joints or nodes. FLOWERS may be white or various shades of pink to red. They may be single or form a cluster or inflorescence. The oldest flowers are in the center. Each bloom is perfect, having both male and female parts. It has five united sepals, five petals, ten stamens, and one pistil composed of two carpels. The ovary matures into a dry, indehiscent FRUIT classified as a capsule.

The pink family is called Caryophyllaceae. Most pinks belong to the genus *Dianthus.*

H. J. C.

Pinna see Ear

Sweet Williams, of the pink family

Pinnate venation see Leaves

Pinworm Pinworms are round, unsegmented worms. The females are about ¼ inch (6 millimeters) long and the males are smaller. They are PARASITES in the human intestine. Pinworm infection is very common in children. A survey made in the United States showed that about 33 per cent of the children were infected.

Pinworms have direct development without a second or *intermediate host.* In the large intestine, males and females are attached to the *epithelial tissue.* After fertilization, females are packed with eggs. They migrate posteriorly at night to lay eggs around the anus, and then return to the upper large intestine. One female may lay 10,000 eggs at a time. The anal region becomes very itchy. Children scratch and pick up eggs under their fingernails. Eggs carried to the mouth on fingernails pass into the digestive tract and hatch in the duodenum. Larvae migrate to the large intestine. When they reach their destination, they are mature worms. This life cycle usually takes two months. If the temperature is cool, eggs deposited on clothing or bedclothing remain alive for about a week.

J. C. K.

SEE ALSO: NEMATHELMINTHES

Piranha see Tropical fish

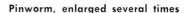

Pinworm, enlarged several times

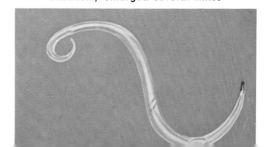

Conversion Factors
to Metric Measurement

Length
1 inch = 25.4 millimeters (mm) exactly
1 inch = 2.54 centimeters (cm) exactly
1 foot = 0.3048 meters (m) exactly
1 yard = 0.9144 meters (m) exactly
1 mile = 1.609344 kilometers (km) exactly

Area
1 square inch = 6.4516 square centimeters (cm^2) exactly
1 square foot = 0.092903 square meters (m^2)
1 square yard = 0.836127 square meters (m^2)
1 square acre = 0.404686 hectares (ha)
1 square mile = 2.58999 square kilometers (km^2)

Cubic Measure
1 cubic inch = 16.387064 cubic centimeters (cm^3) exactly
1 cubic foot = 0.0283168 cubic meters (m^3)
1 cubic yard = 0.764555 cubic meters (m^3)

US Liquid Measure
1 fluid ounce = 29.5735 milliliters (ml)
1 fluid ounce = 0.2957 deciliters (dl)
1 pint = 0.473176 liters (l)
1 gallon = 3.78541 liters (l)

US Dry Measure
1 pint = 0.550610 liters (l)
1 bushel = 35.2391 liters (l)

Weight
1 grain = 0.0647989 grams (g)
1 ounce = 28.3495 grams (g)
1 pound = 0.453592 kilograms (kg)
1 short ton = 0.907185 metric tons (t)
1 UK ton = 1.01605 metric tons (t)

Temperature
To convert Fahrenheit to Centigrade (Celsius) complete the following
equation. $(F° - 32) \times 5 \div 9 = C°$